Using Linguistically Appropriate Practice

D1477402

FSC
www.fsc.org
MIX
Paper from
responsible sources
FSC® C013604

Multilingual Matters publishes books for scholars, students and teachers with a focus on multilingualism, language learning and social justice. The following books can be used to extend the ideas found in this book.

Talking About Global Migration: Implications for Language Teaching by Theresa Catalano

As the world faces a migration crisis, there is an enhanced need for educational responses to the linguistic and cultural diversity of student bodies, and for consideration of migrant students at all levels of the curriculum. This book explores the stories of over 70 migrants from 41 countries around the world and examines the language they use when talking about their move to a new country and their experiences there.

Language Teaching and Learning in a Multilingual World by Marie-Françoise Narcy-Combs et al.

The majority of people around the world live in multilingual societies, and so it follows that plurilingualism should be considered normal. This book proposes a flexible and adaptive framework for designing and implementing language learning environments and tasks, which will be useful for practitioners working in classrooms where many languages are already spoken.

Educating Refugee-background Students: Critical Issues and Dynamic Contexts by Shawna Shapiro et al.

This collection of offers an in-depth exploration of key issues in the education of adolescents and adults with refugee backgrounds residing in North America, Australia and Europe. These studies foreground student goals, experiences and voices, and reflect a high degree of awareness of the assets that refugee-background students bring to schools and broader society.

Twelve Lectures on Multilingualism edited by David Singleton and Larissa Aronin

This textbook offers an accessible introduction to many of the most interesting areas in the study of multilingualism. It consists of twelve lectures, written by leading researchers, each dedicated to a particular topic of importance. Each lecture offers a state-of-the-art, authoritative review of a subdiscipline of the field. The volume sheds light on the ways in which the use and acquisition of languages are changing, providing new insights into the nature of contemporary multilingualism.

Visualising Multilingual Lives: More than Words edited by Paula Kalaja and Sílvia Melo-Pfeifer

This book brings together empirical studies from around the world to help readers gain a better understanding of multilinguals, ranging from small children to elderly people, and their lives.

You can buy these books on our website http://www.multilingual-matters.com and receive a 40% discount using the code LAP40.

Using Linguistically Appropriate Practice

A Guide for Teaching in Multilingual Classrooms

Roma Chumak-Horbatsch

MULTILINGUAL MATTERS
Bristol • Blue Ridge Summit

To Marko

DOI https://doi.org/10.21832/CHUMAK4955

Library of Congress Cataloging in Publication Data
A catalog record for this book is available from the Library of Congress.
Names: Chumak-Horbatsch, Roma, author.
Title: Using Linguistically Appropriate Practice: A Guide for Teaching in Multilingual Classrooms/
    Roma Chumak-Horbatsch.
Description: Blue Ridge Summit, PA: Multilingual Matters, [2019] | Includes bibliographical references
    and index.
Identifiers: LCCN 2019010148 (print) | LCCN 2019018894 (ebook) | ISBN 9781788924962 (pdf) | ISBN
    9781788924979 (epub) | ISBN 9781788924986 (Kindle) | ISBN 9781788924955
    (hbk : alk. paper) | ISBN 9781788924948 (pbk : alk. paper)
Subjects: LCSH: Immigrant children—Education. | Multilingual education. | Education, Bilingual. |
    Multilingualism. | Language and languages—Study and teaching.
Classification: LCC LC3715 (ebook) | LCC LC3715 .C494 2019 (print) | DDC 370.117—dc23
LC record available at https://lccn.loc.gov/2019010148

British Library Cataloguing in Publication Data
A catalogue entry for this book is available from the British Library.

ISBN-13: 978-1-78892-495-5 (hbk)
ISBN-13: 978-1-78892-494-8 (pbk)

Multilingual Matters
UK: St Nicholas House, 31–34 High Street, Bristol BS1 2AW, UK.
USA: NBN, Blue Ridge Summit, PA, USA.

Website: www.multilingual-matters.com
Twitter: Multi_Ling_Mat
Facebook: https://www.facebook.com/multilingualmatters
Blog: www.channelviewpublications.wordpress.com

Copyright © 2019 Roma Chumak-Horbatsch.
™Chumak-Horbatsch, R. (2018)
Trademark application (identifier) number 1885633. Toronto, Ontario, Canada.

TERM: LINGUISTICALLY APPROPRIATE PRACTICE
ACRONYM: LAP

All rights reserved. No part of this work may be reproduced in any form or by any means without
permission in writing from the publisher.

The policy of Multilingual Matters/Channel View Publications is to use papers that are natural,
renewable and recyclable products, made from wood grown in sustainable forests. In the manufacturing
process of our books, and to further support our policy, preference is given to printers that have FSC and
PEFC Chain of Custody certification. The FSC and/or PEFC logos will appear on those books where full
certification has been granted to the printer concerned.

Typeset by Nova Techset Private Limited, Bengaluru and Chennai, India.
Printed and bound in the UK by the CPI Books Group Ltd.
Printed and bound in the US by NBN.

Contents

Acknowledgements

A very special *thank you* to the countless children, teachers, school administrators, settlement workers, university students, families, colleagues, researchers, collaborators and contributors who, in so many different and special ways, made this book happen. Their voices make up the multilingual teaching and learning portrait presented in this book. To all of these I extend a deep and heartfelt thank you.

THANK YOU, MERCI, ДЯКУЮ, GRAZIE, TAK, DANKE, DZIĘKUJĘ, TAKK, KIITOS, ŠUKRAN, GO RAIBH MAITH AGAT, DANK JE, DHANWAAD, XIÈ XIÈ, MAHADSANID, GAMSAHAMNIDA, HVALA, TACK, TÄNAN, MARAMING SALAMAT, EFHARISTO, OBRIGADO, ASANTE, MANANA, GRAZZI, DHANYAWAADH, ARIGATO, KOP KHUN, SPASIBA, NANDRI

Thank you also to Dr Jim Cummins who, over the course of my multilingual journey, was always on hand with resources, suggestions and very good advice. A warm *merci* to Monique Bélanger for her editorial support. Thank you also to Anna Roderick and the Multilingual Matters team. Finally, I would like to thank my husband, Marko, for his support and encouragement. To him I dedicate this book.

Contributors

The students, teachers-in-training, teachers, principals, consultants, authors, researchers and colleagues listed here contributed to the LAP profiles and the LAP resources.

Teachers-in-training

   Jessica Altimari, Paige Badger, Wei Cao Zi, Candice Chan, Lan Chan, Tegan Chan, Jessy Choi, Christina Cinelli, Jessica Cipparrone, Allison Diolanda, Ikram Dirie, Sarah Maggie El'Lithy, Humaira Gharayia, Sharon Hartman, Eunice Joo, Christie Leung, Camila Macdonald, An Mai, Marta Masnij, Adizat Ofulue, Alfie Ogalesco, Lasheka Packkiyarajah, Lubomyr Stasyszyn, Meaghan Sullivan, Iqura Tariq and Zhen Wang Qiao.

Bobby Abrol, PhD, started her career as an elementary school teacher. She worked extensively for the development of teacher education curriculum and also taught as a teacher educator in India. Currently, Bobby works for Tata Trusts, a philanthropic organization in India. Her work portfolio includes policy and advocacy in teacher education in India through active deliberation with the government.

Jenni Alisaari, PhD, is a university teacher and a multilingual researcher from the University of Turku in Finland. She started her career as a music and language teacher (English and Finnish). For Jenni, combining language learning and singing has always been natural. Children's excitement and enthusiasm showed her how singing engages all learners, helps them learn vocabulary, language structures and phrases, and improves their oral ability. Currently, Jenni works in teacher education and trains future teachers to use singing in language teaching along with other pedagogical methods.

Helen Arnold has three passions – languages, teaching and travelling. She has lived and worked in Russia, Belarus, the USA, South Korea, Slovakia and Germany and is a speaker of five languages. Helen has worked in international schools promoting International Baccalaureate values such as international mindedness, respect, curiosity and the celebration of languages and cultures. Helen describes the children in her multilingual classrooms as 'intercultural experts' who have much to share and offer. Families and the entire school community participate in Helen's multilingual agenda.

Fríða Bjarney Jónsdóttir started her career as a preschool teacher. She then worked as an assistant principal and principal in Lækjaborg, a preschool in Reykjavík, Iceland. A strong advocate of multilingual teaching, Fríða initiated a multicultural preschool practices project and participated in a number of research projects that focus on diversity, inclusion and social justice. Fríða shares her passion for multilingual pedagogy with teachers and teachers-in-training. She is a lecturer in teacher education at the University of Iceland. Her current work includes being a project coordinator and consultant for multicultural education in preschools in the Department of Education and Youth in Reykjavík. In her PhD thesis, Fríða focuses on practices with linguistically and culturally diverse preschool children.

Gillian Caron is the vice-principal of an elementary school in Ontario. She has worked with many newcomer children, encouraging them to document and share their personal stories. She is inspired to see all children grow and succeed. Gillian identifies equity and inclusion as her teaching guideposts.

Roberto Di Prospero began his teaching career supporting students with learning differences. He quickly saw that many of the teaching strategies that apply to this population are also important in supporting newcomers. Roberto views children from an asset perspective and is responsive to their strengths and needs. As a school principal, Roberto has collaborated with Jim Cummins and Roma Chumak-Horbatsch on a number of research projects. For Roberto, the arrival of over 100 Syrian newcomers in his school was a professional highlight. Working with these children and families reaffirmed the moral and pedagogical power of multilingual teaching.

Lynn Desharnais has over 20 years' teaching experience. She is currently a teacher-librarian and a part-time English as a second language teacher. She works with a team of special education and English language teachers to support the language and literacy needs of newcomers.

Eithne Gallagher (www.eithnegallagher.net) is a recognized authority in the field of multilingualism in international education. She has chaired the European Council of International Schools English-as-a-second language and mother-tongue committee. She is a regular presenter at conferences and delivers workshops and lectures for teachers, administrators and parents across the world. Her work has been widely published in educational journals and magazines. Her book, *Equal Rights to the Curriculum: Many Languages, One Message*, argues for school reform to meet the educational needs of all children growing up in a multilingual, multicultural society. Eithne provides support and consultancy for schools planning to implement inclusive language policies. Eithne's most recent work, *The Glitterlings*, is a story-based early years programme, published by Oxford University Press in 2015.

Meagan Geddes was born in South Africa and moved to Ontario, Canada when she was a teenager. She has always wanted to be involved in inspiring children to be lifelong learners. She strongly believes that if all children are provided with the right entry point into their learning, they will flourish. Meagan completed a diploma in early learning and has taught various grades in the elementary school. She has developed a programme that allows children to learn in safe and meaningful environments.

Sonja Grcic-Stuart has worked as a high school teacher of English and also as an English as an additional language teacher in Quebec City and in Halifax, Canada. She currently leads the English as an additional language programme for the Halifax Regional School Board, the largest school board in Atlantic Canada, serving 48,000 students in 136 schools. Sonja is the author of several Canadian educational resource books in a science and social studies series to support language learning in the content areas. The focus of Sonja's work is supporting newcomers, helping them integrate into their new school and manage the curriculum. She is a strong advocate of multilingual pedagogy and works closely with teachers, families and communities to ensure student success.

Leena Maria Heikkola started her teaching career in a Finnish village called Salolampi. She has also taught Finnish to three- to seven-year-olds at the Brisbane-Finnish School in Brisbane, Australia and to adults at the universities of Helsinki and Turku. Leena Maria uses singing as part of her language and culture teaching.

Anita Isaksson worked as a principal in primary schools in the Borlänge municipality in Sweden for 10 years. During that time she coordinated and developed a multilingual programme to integrate and teach newly arrived students. Anita was also involved in international projects with primary schools in Great Britain and Canada. She retired in 2017.

Allison Kennedy is an experienced teacher with more than 15 years in kindergarten and early elementary classrooms. She has extensive experience in special education and English language learning, and has worked in linguistically diverse communities. Allison is a frequent workshop presenter on language topics. In 2017 Allison secured funding for a literacy project. With her team of early childhood educators and speech-language pathologists, she uses literacy instruction to support kindergarten children's learning. Currently, Allison works in the Kindergarten Early Language Intervention (KELI) programme at the Toronto District School Board, working alongside speech-language pathologists to support children with special oral language and literacy needs.

Claudine Kirsch started her career as a primary school teacher in Luxembourg. She completed her Masters and PhD in education at Goldsmiths, University of London, where she worked as a lecturer from 2003 to 2011. She is currently associate professor in the Faculty of Language and Literature, Humanities, Arts and Education at the University of Luxembourg and a member of the Institute for Research in Multilingualism.

Her research interests include foreign and second language learning and teaching, multilingualism, multilingual pedagogies, translanguaging, family language policies and language learner strategies. She is the principal investigator of two projects: iTEO (2013–2017) and MuLiPEC (Developing Multilingual Pedagogies in Early Childhood; 2016–2019). She also takes part in the project CALIDIE (Capitalising on Linguistic Diversity in Education; 2017–2022).

Paula Markus is a sessional lecturer specializing in supporting English language learners at the Ontario Institute for Studies in Education of the University of Toronto. She enjoyed a 30-year teaching career with the Toronto District School Board: as a secondary school ESL/ELD teacher, department head and as the ESL/ELD programme coordinator for the board. Paula is particularly proud of the Toronto District School Board's extensive LEAP programme for newcomer students with limited prior schooling, and of the impressive gains that students in this programme have made in closing the gaps in their academic backgrounds resulting from interrupted formal schooling due to war, refugee camp living and other challenges on their way to life in Canada. Paula has served on a number of Ontario Ministry of Education curriculum writing teams, and has been an invited presenter at conferences in Canada, the USA and Europe.

Kristen McGinn has worked with newcomer children and families as both a classroom teacher and an English as a second language support teacher. Kristen is a strong advocate of children's home languages. For her, children's home languages affect their identity formation and their self-confidence. Kristen describes herself as a lifelong learner. She reflects on and extends her professional practice by keeping social justice at the forefront of her teaching.

Suzanne Muir is an educator and equity and inclusion consultant. She is a published children's author dedicated to multilingual and culturally responsive teaching.

Bonny Norton, PhD, FRSC, is a professor and Distinguished University Scholar in the Department of Language and Literacy Education at the University of British Columbia (Canada). Her primary research interests are identity and language learning, critical literacy and international development. Her current projects address open access digital resources for multilingual children. She is research lead of Storybooks Canada (http://www.storybookscanada.ca/; http://faculty.educ.ubc.ca/norton/).

Marina Petrovic is an elementary English as a second language teacher with a passion for building inclusive classrooms. She draws on her own experiences as a newcomer and provides leadership for teachers to build their capacity in understanding their diverse learners.

Serena Quintal is a core French teacher. She is inspired every day by the cultural and linguistic diversity of her students. Through her current graduate studies in language and literacies education at the Ontario Institute for Studies in Education (Toronto), Serena is exploring effective pedagogy which advocates for cultural and linguistic diversity in French as a second language programmes. Serena has shared her work in resource development at the Ontario Modern Language Teachers' Association Conference, and also at the annual Celebrating Linguistic Diversity Conference in Toronto.

Charlene Ryan, PhD, is an elementary early childhood music specialist in Toronto, Canada. She currently serves as director of the School of Early Childhood Studies at Ryerson University, with previous posts at the Berklee College of Music in Boston, USA and McGill University in Montreal, Canada. In addition to her teaching experience (at grade school and university level), she has developed successful community music education programmes for children and continues to work with toddlers and preschoolers in the Early Learning Centre at Ryerson University. Charlene is the author of *Building Strong Music Programs: A Handbook for Pre-service and Novice Music Teachers*, a *Choice Magazine* Outstanding Academic Title. She has researched and published widely on the performance experiences of young musicians, with a focus on performance anxiety.

Debbie Samson is a passionate educator who deeply believes in the importance of first language development, multilingual pedagogy and linguistic diversity. Early on in her career as an English as a second language teacher, Debbie saw many shortcomings in traditional programmes. In her teaching she worked with students and families, bringing their languages into the school and transforming her practice. Today she refers to herself as a multilingual language learner and she works with others to develop and implement multilingual pedagogical strategies. Debbie holds a graduate degree in language, culture and teaching. In all that she does, Debbie creates spaces for the voices of students and their families to be heard and acted upon. Debbie is the recipient of a variety of educational awards, including the Elementary Teachers Federation of Ontario Rainbow Teachers Award (2015), the South African Women to Women Education Award (2005) and the Ellen Becker Award for outstanding work in the area of language and literacy (2000).

Angélique Sanders has over 28 years of experience working with young children and mentoring student educators at Ryerson University's School of Early Childhood Studies. Her love of languages fuelled her multilingual teaching early on in her career. Angélique has collaborated with Roma Chumak-Horbatsch on various LAP projects across the city of Toronto. Angélique is a language advocate and activist. She pays attention to the languages of children, families, student educators, colleagues, community members and visitors. In 2013 Angélique received the Canadian Prime Minister's Award of Excellence in Early Childhood Education for her outstanding multilingual teaching.

Safiya Shere has worked as a classroom teacher, an English as a second language teacher and an English literacy development teacher. Collaboration and collegiality are important for Safiya. She works closely with her teaching team to support newcomers, including those who have had their schooling interrupted.

Angelpreet Singh completed her BA in early childhood education at Ryerson University, as well as a BEd and MEd in language, culture and teaching from York University. She is currently a PhD candidate in the languages, cultures and literacies programme in the Faculty of Education at Simon Fraser University in British Columbia, Canada. Angelpreet's dissertation focuses on young Punjabi-speaking children and the literacy practices adopted in early learning settings.

Reena Soin is a teacher in a linguistically diverse downtown Toronto elementary school. Drawing on 20 years of professional experience, she creates a welcoming and inclusive classroom environment in which students feel valued, respected and successful. Reena creates her own resources and adopts strategies to support newcomers as they build upon their prior knowledge and linguistic assets.

Saga Stephensen completed her undergraduate degree in Icelandic and Japanese in 2007 and a graduate degree in Japanese studies from the School of Oriental and African Studies in London in 2009. During her time in London, Saga worked as a secondary school teacher. She lived in Japan from 2012 to 2014 and completed a graduate degree in migration and intercultural studies, focusing on intercultural education. She is currently working as head teacher in Miðborg, a linguistically diverse preschool in Reykjavik, Iceland, where the children speak 21 different home languages. She is also leading a Miðborg multilingual pilot project called Magical Languages.

Susan Stuckless has taught kindergarten through to Grade 5. She is currently working as both an English as a second language and a special education teacher in an Ontario school. Susan's love of languages comes from living in Montreal (Canada) as a child, and having bilingual conversations with her father. These language experiences help Susan connect with and understand newcomers.

Kelleen Toohey, PhD, is Professor Emerita at Simon Fraser University, Vancouver, BC, Canada. She has published in the area of minority language education, English language learning and teaching, and recently, explores how new materialism might expand our views of language education research and pedagogy ('The onto-epistemologies of new materialism: Implications for applied linguistics research and pedagogy', *Applied Linguistics*, 2019). Her recently published second edition of *Learning English at School: Identity, Socio-material Relations and Classroom Practice* (Multilingual Matters, 2018) provides an example of how an ethnography of young language learners, originally analyzed through sociocultural theory, might be re-interpreted through new materialist concepts.

Drífa Þórarinsdóttir has extensive experience in teaching young children. She has worked as both a preschool teacher and a principal. Drífa holds both a MEd and a diploma in special education. She is currently enrolled in a collaborative graduate parent education program at the Universities of Iceland and Minnesota. Drífa was a project manager of a literacy project, Leikskólalæsi, in Kindergarten Kiðagil. She also has wide experience in teaching bilingual children and working with families. Currently Drífa is head of Kindergarten Tröllaborgir in Akureyri, Iceland.

Gina Valle, PhD, focuses on the intersectionality of culture, language and identity. She is the author of *Teachers at Their Best – Enseignants sous leur meilleur jour* and, with the support of UNESCO, is the editor and publisher of the multilingual children's book *The Best of all Worlds – Le meilleur monde imaginable*.

Anneli Wessman has worked as a kindergarten teacher and a primary school teacher for over 30 years. She is currently a lead teacher, a school developer and a Swedish as a second language teacher in Borlänge Municipality, Sweden. She works at Välkomstcentrum, Borlänge Municipality's welcoming centre, conducting orientation interviews and assessments of newcomers between the ages of seven and 19. Anneli also mentors teachers' collegial learning circles. Her areas of interest include multilingual education, supporting multilingual students' academic progress in all subjects, multilingual literacy development, and practical approaches to affirming identities in multilingual contexts. Anneli has initiated school development projects as well as international projects with schools in Great Britain and Canada. Anneli keeps up to date on multilingual recourses and presents at workshops and conferences.

Tracy Wheatley-Romano is an instructional programme leader with the Halton District School Board in Ontario (Canada). Her portfolio includes elementary English as a second language lead where she supports a team of 70 teachers. This team helps newcomers across Halton connect to one another using their first languages. Tracy continues to promote these collaborative and connecting opportunities, focusing on the transitions of Grade 8 and 9 new arrivals.

Rahat Zaidi, PhD is an Associate Professor in Second Language Pedagogy at the Faculty of Education, University of Calgary, in Alberta, Canada. She works with school boards and pre-service teacher education programs as well as political stakeholders and policy makers in Alberta and beyond. The focus of her work is to: create awareness of the benefits of bilingualism and multilingualism; broaden the framework of second language pedagogy to include application for mainstream schools, and create a language awareness curriculum for schools.

Tobin Zikmanis brings out the best in all children. In his work with newcomers, he builds on and extends what they know and love. He uses technology to connect with newcomers and helps them integrate into the classroom, participate in the curriculum and take control of their own learning. For Tobin, the following matter most in his teaching: collaboration, patience, empathy, and the understanding that we are all lifelong learners.

Foreword

Roma Chumak-Horbatsch's extraordinary new book, *Using Linguistically Appropriate Practice: A Guide for Teaching in Multilingual Classrooms* builds on and extends her 2012 Linguistically Appropriate Practice: A Guide for Working with Young Immigrant Children. Together they provide blueprints for pedagogical practice in classrooms with not only young immigrant learners, but as Jim Cummins observed about the first book, they concern educationally appropriate practice for the diverse classrooms of today in many countries.

The recommendation that school instruction for minority students be more closely tied to the cultural and linguistic practices of students' homes and communities is not new (Cazden *et al.*, 1972; Heath, 1983; Muspratt *et al.*, 1997; Orellana & Reynolds, 2008, among many others). In the early 1950s, UNESCO produced a position paper stating, 'We take it as axiomatic... that the best medium for teaching is the mother tongue of the pupil' (UNESCO, 1953: 6). In the 1970s, along with growing educational interest in the field of sociolinguistics, many scholars documented and lamented how the language and literacy practices of schooling ignored, attempted to remediate and/or devalued the cultures and languages of non-white, non-middle-class and non-English speaking students and their families (Cazden, 1970; Philips, 1972; Michell-Kernan, 1972; and many others). In the 1980s, Heath's (1983) ground-breaking ten-year ethnography of language use in three American communities showed that some communities' language and literacy practices aligned better with those valued in schools, and to the extent that children came from communities with the same or different language and literacy conventions, they were advantaged or disadvantaged in schooling. Subsequently, many studies documented various differences (and their consequences) in language and literacy practices in various communities (e.g. Michaels, 1981). Projects with non-official-language-speaking Indigenous students in Mexico and on the Navajo Reservation in the Southwest U.S. showed very promising results for children initially educated in their home languages and later learning an official language (Modiano, 1973; Roessell, 1977; McCarty, 1987). Projects in which Finnish immigrant (to Sweden) students were educated in Finnish before later transitioning to Swedish-medium schools, also showed very good second language learning results (Skuttnabb-Kangas & Toukomaa, 1976). This work was conducted in Indigenous and other racially minoritized communities and with participants of varying social classes, but only rarely in situations where immigrant or refugee children came to school with a variety of language codes and practices, so that mother tongue education for all would have been impractical.

Geo-political conflicts, environmental catastrophes, and integrated international economies, have in the 2000s, all been major factors in the increasing physical and virtual movements of people across national boundaries. Some newcomers come with privileges and resources that ease their transitions, but many do not, and newcomers' mastery of the official language(s) of their new homes is often seen as prerequisite to their participation in those countries' cultural, educational, political, and economic institutions. Typically, the languages newcomers bring are seen to inhibit official language learning. For Roma, as for many of us involved in language and literacy education, the languages refugees and immigrants bring are resources that are too often squandered in 'integration' attempts. She states unequivocally: 'Monolingual practices do not work in linguistically diverse classrooms' (p. 2), and she recognizes that we need to think about and act differently in the classrooms of today. Moreover, she not only espouses the long-held view that all languages are assets, she also tells us ways this view can be incorporated into classroom practice.

This much-to-be-welcomed book reports on the implementation of Linguistically Appropriate Practice (LAP), developed and articulated by Roma, in diverse settings (with over 100 professionals in 15 countries!). The exciting and imaginative ways teachers have taken up LAP that are reported here must be due in large part to the reader-friendly accessibility of her first book which, like this one, masterfully explains relevant research and its implications for practice. The current book is replete with stories that illustrate theoretical points and put research findings into context. Stories are often the way teachers describe their practice, and anthropologists Carolyn Gatt and Tim Ingold (2013: 147) argued that generative stories should be 'generous, open-ended, comparative yet critical inquir[ies] into the conditions and potential of human life'. Certainly, the stories Roma tells, reporting on diverse educational settings, bring to readers' attention exciting possibilities for making classrooms more welcoming to multilingual (and other) students, and at the same time, perhaps more satisfying and more interesting for teachers. The wealth of knowledge, beliefs, religions, literature and so on of multilingual students and their families are often given lip service in educational discourse, but rarely do we find reports of pedagogical practices that instantiate this perspective. This book shows in stories and photographs how linguistically and culturally appropriate practice has been taken up in diverse sites, with the kind of detail that will encourage teachers and other readers to imagine how they might put these ideas into action in the sites for which they have responsibility. Developing nuanced and sophisticated understandings of the cultural and linguistic diversity that surrounds us all, is important in education in the widest possible sense.

Roma and I were doctoral students together at the Ontario Institute for Studies in Education (now University of Toronto) in the late 1970s and early 1980s. Her interests and background in early childhood education and in bilingual education and child-rearing were apparent then as they are now, as were and are her commitments to teachers and children. Raising her own children multilingually, and working with early childhood educators for many years, Roma definitely has personal experience with the possibilities but also the challenges of LAP. Ending the book with a compilation of resources for teachers and families illustrates Roma's generousity: she is passionate about educational and family practices that foster linguistic plurality, and she is comprehensive in making explicit much of what she knows that can help in that goal. I am pleased and honoured to recommend this book without reservation to teachers, teacher educators, ECE instructors and families who share her commitments.

Kelleen Toohey PhD
Professor Emerita
Faculty of Education
Simon Fraser University
Vancouver, British Columbia, Canada

References

Cazden, C. (1970) Children's questions: Their forms, functions and roles in education. *Young Children* 25, 202–220.

Cazden, C., John, V. and Hymes, D. (eds) (1972) *Functions of Language in the Classroom*. New York: Teachers College Press.

Chumak-Horbatsch, R. (2012) *Linguistically Appropriate Practice: A Guide for Working With Young Immigran tChildren*. Toronto: University of Toronto Press.

Orellana, M.F. and Reynolds, J. (2008) Cultural modeling: Leveraging bilingual skills for school paraphrasing tasks. *Reading Research Quarterly* 43 (1), 48–65.

Gatt, C. and Ingold, T. (2013) From description to correspondence: Anthropology in real time. In W. Gunn, T. Otto and R. Smith (eds) *Design Anthropology: Theory and Practice* (pp. 139–158). London: Bloomsbury Academic.

Heath, S.B. (1983) *Ways with Words: Language, Life and Work in Communities and Classrooms*. Cambridge: Cambridge University Press.

McCarty, T. (1987) The Rough Rock Demonstration School: A case history with implications for educational evaluation. *Human Organization* 46 (2), 103–112.

Michaels, S. (1981) "Sharing time": Children's narrative styles and differential access to literacy. *Language in Society* 10 (3), 423–442.

Muspratt, S., Luke, A. & Freebody, P. (eds) (1997) *Constructing Critical Literacies*. Creskill, NJ: Hampton Press.

Michell-Kernan, C. (1972) On the status of Black English for native speakers: An assessment of attitudes and values. In C. Cazden, V. John and D. Hymes (eds) *Functions of Language in the Classroom* (pp. 195–210). New York: Teachers College Press.

Modiano, N. (1973) *Indian Education in the Chiapas Highlands*. New York: Holt, Rinehart and Winston.

Philips, S.U. (1972) Participant structures and communicative competence: Warm Springs children in community and classroom. In C. Cazden, V. John and D. Hymes, D. (eds) *Functions of Language in the Classroom* (pp. 370–394). New York: Teachers College Press.

Roessell, R. (1977) *Navajo Education in Action*. Chinle, AZ: Navajo Curriculum Centre, Rough Rock Demonstration School.

Skuttnabb-Kangas, T. and Toukomaa, P. (1976) *Teaching Migrant Children's Mother Tongue and Learning the Language of the Host Country in the Context of the Socio-Cultural Situation of the Migrant Family*. Paris: UNESCO.

UNESCO (1953) *The Use of Vernacular Languages in Education*. Paris: UNESCO.

Introduction

The Number Five

5

The number five somehow became a part of this book. Five is not my lucky number (three is), nor that of Monique, my trusted editor (she goes for nine). Yet five appears throughout the book you are holding in your hands.

Here's how it all started. During my many visits to schools and childcare centres I often saw children and teachers approach each other, shout 'gimme five' or 'high five', and slap raised palms in greeting, acknowledgement or celebration. I soon became a part of this **g5** happy practice and often wondered where it had originated and why it is so popular with children.

A quick Google search revealed that the **g5** hand gesture originated from the 'low five' (the opposite of 'gimme five' or 'high five'), and has been a part of African American culture since WWII. I also learned that 'gimme five' has been used by volleyball and baseball players since 1960. A lover of words and phrases, I was especially interested to learn that 'gimme five' entered the Oxford English Dictionary 38 years ago!

Why is **g5** popular with children? It is a quick and safe way to connect with others, communicate acceptance and friendship and share happiness, success and joy. I noted that even newcomers, children new to the school language, quickly and proudly adopt the 'gimme five' practice.

So how did five find its way into this book? The answer is quite simple. This book comes five years after the publication of the original LAP book (Chumak-Horbatsch, 2012; hereafter referred to as LAP12). It is based on five LAP actions I conducted over a five-year period. My hope is that this book will provide you with five important take-away messages.

Chumak-Horbatsch, R. (2012) *Linguistically Appropriate Practice: A Guide for Working with Young Immigrant Children.* Toronto: University of Toronto Press. With a Foreword by Dr Jim Cummins.

This guidebook is an introduction to linguistically appropriate practice. It is intended for teachers and professionals who work with young children who do not speak the language of programme delivery. It introduces LAP, explains why a new instructional practice is important, and provides suggestions and activities for transforming classrooms into multilingual learning environments.

Five Years Ago

Five years ago, in response to numerous requests from teachers working with children with little (or no) command of the language of programme delivery, I developed and published LAP12, a teaching practice that I called **Linguistically Appropriate Practice or LAP.** LAP invites teachers to open their doors to children's home languages, integrate them into the new language environment, support and nurture their growing bilingualism, help them learn the school language and meet their unique language and literacy needs.

Five Years Later

Since its publication, LAP12 has become the 'go to' resource for teachers working with newcomer children in Canada, the United States, European and Nordic countries, Australia and Japan. LAP12 is used in childcare centres, preschool groups, family literacy groups, kindergartens and primary level (Grades 1–3) classrooms. It has also been adapted for junior and intermediate level classrooms (Grades 4–8) and numerous language learning and intervention programmes. LAP12 has found its way into professional book clubs and staff meetings. It is the topic of sharing and discussion at multilingual workshops and conferences. LAP12 has been translated into Greek to help teachers working in Greece integrate newcomer children. Also, a number of undergraduate education courses and teacher training programmes have adopted LAP12 as required or supplemental reading for diversity and curriculum courses.

A Five-year Follow-up LAP Journey

Shortly after the publication of LAP12, I set out on a follow-up, fact-finding journey. This journey lasted five years and included five professional actions (Table 0.1). During that time I collaborated with colleagues, researchers, students, children, families, authors and school administrators in 15 countries.

In addition to the five professional actions, I embarked on a personal language-learning journey. I wanted to better understand what it means to be 'new' to a language and to be

Table 0.1 Five fact-finding actions

Professional actions	Activities
Fieldwork	• visits to childcare centres, classrooms and specialized programmes; • interactions and collaboration with children, families, community members, children's book authors, teachers and school librarians; • communication with colleagues, teachers, educational researchers and authors of children's books; • demonstration lessons in childcare centres and classrooms.
Presentations	• presentation of LAP at multilingual conferences, workshops, staff meetings, and parent groups.
Launch and supervision of LAP	• trained coaches to support and facilitate the implementation of LAP in early learning contexts. • LAP launched in: – a Toronto kindergarten school with an enrolment of 700; – three childcare centres with an enrolment of 140 children and 30 teachers. • LAP internships: undergraduate and graduate students implemented LAP in childcare centres, classrooms (kindergarten to Grade 5) and special programmes.
A new course	• development of a new course entitled 'Childhood Bilingualism' which has been added to the undergraduate programme of study at the School of Early Childhood Studies at Ryerson University.
Publications	• contributions to classroom and school newsletters, blogs, websites, language policy and language curriculum documents; • journal article (Chumak-Horbatsch & Chung, 2016); • book chapter (Chumak-Horbatsch, 2017).

surrounded by a stream of unknown speech. I decided to learn Italian. Why Italian? The answer is simple: Italian is the language of opera and I love opera. Five years later, I am still a learner of Italian. I have experienced a wide range of emotions in the learning of my new language. These include the following:

• success: when I make progress;
• pride: acknowledgement and praise from the teacher, 'Brava, Roma';
• excitement: learning something new, for example how the prefix 's' creates opposites in select words – fortuna = luck, sfortuna = bad luck;
• joy: reading my first Italian novel without a dictionary;
• confusion: not understanding a grammar point;
• frustration: forgetting recently learned words;
• embarrassment: responding incorrectly in class when all eyes are on me; and
• anxiety: determination to get it 'right'.

During my LAP fact-finding journey I recorded all that I witnessed, observed, encountered, heard and overheard. My documentation trove included detailed field notes, photographs, video-clips, audio-recordings, samples of children's work, journal entries, evaluations and resource lists.

The purpose of my LAP journey was threefold:

• to witness LAP 'in action' and gauge the extent of its adoption and implementation;
• to become a language learner and better understand newcomers; and

- to share my experiences and findings, to provide continued support to those who have adopted LAP and to encourage others to consider retooling their practice and opening their classroom doors to languages.

About This Book

The book you are holding in your hands is the outcome of my LAP journey. It is written in the same reader-friendly style and format as LAP12. It is an updated and extended portrait of LAP and is based on voices from the field: collaborations with over 100 professionals from 15 countries. It includes testimonials, reflection and experiences from over 30 contributors from five countries who, at the time of writing, were engaged in various aspects of multilingual teaching.

Whether you are new to LAP or are a veteran of multilingual teaching, this book will help you create and sustain a classroom environment that is inclusive, multilingual, engaging and exciting. Use this book as an add-on to your existing curriculum. Adapt, adjust and extend what you read to match your teaching context, your grade level and the learning needs of the children.

Using this book

The five chapters can be read as they are presented, or you can read them in the order that best meets your needs. Taken together, they provide a picture of LAP: what it is; how it plays out in classrooms; and tips and strategies for moving your multilingual agenda forward.

Read the book on your own or with a colleague. Organize a professional book club in your school, and meet regularly with your colleagues to talk about multilingual teaching, share ideas and collaborate on activities. The five topics found in the 'Consider this …' section at the end of each chapter are intended for group reflection and discussion. Here is a summary of the five chapters.

Chapter 1: LAP Basics

The first chapter provides essential information about LAP. To simplify your reading, terms used throughout the book are defined. Following this, five reasons for adopting multilingual teaching are presented. You will also find an easy-to-read discussion of the learning and bilingual theories that support LAP. If you are new to LAP this chapter will serve as an introduction. If you are a LAP teacher it will help you strengthen your understanding of multilingual teaching.

Chapter 2: LAP Teachers

This chapter looks at LAP teachers – who they are, what they do and why they do it. LAP teachers are committed to multilingual teaching. They reject the 'silent period' and challenge the idea of silent newcomers. LAP teachers are tuned into children's needs and understand their different and unique 'learning agendas'. As 'guides on the side', they challenge and support all children and ensure their engagement in 'rich tasks'. To guide and assess children's skills and learning, LAP teachers adopt dynamic assessment, an interactive technique that focuses on the process of learning rather than on the measurement of isolated skills. LAP teachers rely on technological support to integrate newcomers, help with translations and engage all children in the curriculum.

Chapter 3: LAP Profiles

LAP comes to life in this chapter. The profiles include LAP journeys, where teachers and teachers-in-training share their personal insights on multilingual teaching. Also included in the profiles are reports on how LAP has been implemented in schools and specialized educational programmes.

Chapter 4: LAP Challenges

This chapter explores and explains four challenges identified by LAP teachers. These include strategies for engaging *all* children in LAP activities, encouraging newcomers to use their home languages in the classroom, supporting children who are single speakers of little known languages and partnering with families.

Chapter 5: LAP Resources

The last chapter introduces the LAP guide, a six-point tool to help you identify, position and plan your multilingual work. You will also find ideas and tips to enrich and extend your LAP agenda. These include suggestions for organizing a professional book club, book lists, websites, LAP activities, resources for families, reading lists and tips for adding singing to your multilingual agenda.

Getting Started

Are you ready to start (or continue) your multilingual teaching journey? If so, then turn the page and begin!

References

Chumak-Horbatsch, R. (2012) *Linguistically Appropriate Practice: A Guide for Working with Young Immigrant Children*. Toronto: University of Toronto Press.

Chumak-Horbatsch, R. (2017) Instructional practice with young bilingual learners: A Canadian profile. In N. Cabrera and B. Leyendecker (eds) *Handbook on Positive Development of Minority Children*. Cham: Springer.

Chumak-Horbatsch, R. and Chung, L. (2016) C'mon in ... and welcome! Supporting newcomers in Canadian child care centres. *Interaction* 30 (2), 13–16.

1 LAP Basics

Working Definitions

Children in linguistically diverse learning contexts

A linguistically diverse learning context includes children with different language backgrounds: some are newcomers, others are monolinguals and some are bilinguals. Let's have a closer look.

- *Newcomers: Learners of a 'new' language.* Terms of reference for children who arrive in classrooms with little or no command of the school language remain uneven and varied across countries and contexts (Cummins & Early, 2011). In most cases, education policy and curriculum documents are used as guides, and newcomers are identified and labelled as learners of the school language. Here are two examples: in Ontario (Canada) the term English language learners (ELLs) is used, whereas in Sweden new arrivals are referred to as Swedish as a second language learners (SSLLs).

  New arrivals have also been referred to as *emergent bilinguals* (García *et al.*, 2008). Promoted by New York based bilingual researcher Ofelia García, this term accurately describes children's ability to navigate and manage a new language, extend their language repertoire and 'emerge' or grow bilingually. Although widely used by bilingual researchers, this term remains unknown to most teachers.

  In preparing this book I was aware of the limits and inequity of identifying children as learners of the majority or the school language. For this reason, I use the term 'newcomer'. Here's why.

  The 'new' in 'newcomer' refers to the *language* children encounter, making them 'comers' to a 'new' or different language. The term 'newcomer' is simple, inclusive and temporary. It focuses on children's encounter with a 'new' language, regardless of their immigration status, country of birth, country of origin or home language situation. As they navigate their new environment and manage the school language they will, with time, discard the newcomer status and become, to various degrees, bilingual – managing both home and school languages.

- *Monolinguals: speakers of the school language.* Monolingual children are speakers only of the school language.
- *Bilinguals: navigating two languages.* Multilingual classrooms also include bilinguals or children who manage two or more languages. It is important to remember that the actual use of two languages varies significantly across bilingual children. Many start out as newcomers and over time they learn the school language, continue to use their home language and become active bilinguals. Others show preference for the school language, move away from their home language and become passive bilinguals.

Linguistically appropriate practice

- LAP is an approach to teaching in linguistically diverse learning contexts. It invites teachers to reflect on their current practice, let go of 'tried and true' monolingual teaching and respond to the diversity of their classrooms. LAP views newcomers as creative and competent learners, acknowledges and builds on their language and literacy skills and helps them engage with the curriculum.
- LAP is also known as multilingual teaching, teaching through a multilingual lens (Cummins & Persad, 2014), linguistically responsive teaching, and humanizing pedagogy (Salazar, 2013). In this book the term LAP is used interchangeably with multilingual teaching.
- LAP was originally developed as an instructional practice to be used with newcomers or children who are new to the school language. However, my follow-up journey quickly and clearly showed me that LAP is for everyone. It supplements and enriches the prescribed curriculum and extends everyone's knowledge about world language and literacies.
- In LAP classrooms, thinking shifts from the local to the global, and the understanding of 'other' is enhanced. LAP helps *all* children develop 'intercultural understanding' and 'international mindedness' (Gallagher, 2008) and prepares them for the globalized, interconnected world in which they will live and work. A summary of LAP can be found in Table 1.1.

The main features of LAP

> 'At the heart of international mindedness is a frame of mind: a curiosity about the world, an openness towards things "other" and a profound appreciation of the complexity of our world and our relationship to each other.'
>
> M. Bostwick
> Director, Katoh Gakuen Bilingual School, Japan

A central feature of LAP is contact with and interaction between languages and literacies. The LAP teacher creates spaces for home languages and literacies both in the classroom agenda and in all subject areas. In these spaces home languages are

Table 1.1 LAP at a glance

LAP: Background
The Language Portrait shows us that immigrant children: • are emergent bilinguals; • have language lives beyond the classroom; • can successfully navigate two (or more) languages; • have dual-language and literacy needs; • often risk losing their home languages; • experience isolation, loneliness and language shock; and • often remain silent and hide their home languages.
Three different kinds of practices are currently used with immigrant children: • *Assimilative*: Monolingual focus: teaching and learning the school language. • *Supportive*: Monolingual focus with acknowledgement of home languages. • *Inclusive*: Multilingual focus and the promotion of multilingualism and multi-literacy.
What is LAP? • an inclusive, multilingual instructional practice for linguistically diverse classrooms; • views immigrant children as far more than learners of the school language; • builds on their language and literacy skills; and • is grounded in dynamic bilingualism, a theory that focuses on bilinguals' unique language use.

Setting the stage for LAP
Prepare the classroom for LAP: • Take the LAP challenge: commit to multilingual teaching. • Create a language policy: a set of rules to guide classroom language behaviours. • Collect information about children's languages and home literacy practices. • Showcase home languages in charts and graphs. • Create a centre where languages are explored, discovered, compared and shared. • Ensure that classroom displays reflect children's language backgrounds. • Add multilingual music to your classroom agenda.
Transition immigrant children into their new language environment: • Involve the entire class in welcoming activities and discussions. • Encourage family members to spend time in the classroom and use their home language. • Pair newcomers with children who speak the same home language.
Partner with newcomer families: • Inform parents about LAP. • Create a Language Committee that will help with translations and multi-literacy activities. • Share bilingualism resources with families.

LAP activities: Themes and sample activities	
Theme 1: Charting home languages	• Prepare a 'Sign In' book and encourage children to make their own unique entries. • Create a Language Tree with multilingual greetings on cut-out leaves.
Theme 2: Home languages in the classroom	• Invite parents to share simple songs in their home languages. • Encourage children to create bilingual greeting cards for special people and days.
Theme 3: Linking home and classroom	• Discuss mealtime practices across languages and cultures. What happens in your home? • Telephone talk across languages and cultures. How do you answer the phone?
Theme 4: Bring in the outside	• Celebrate International Mother Language Day on 21 February. • Compare environmental sounds across languages (cat, dog, rooster, ambulance).
Theme 5: Sharing books and newspapers	• Start a classroom multilingual newspaper and then extend to a school-wide initiative. • Invite children to create their own dual-language books.

'normalized' as children learn together, use languages 'side-by-side' (García *et al.*, 2017), translate, translanguage, compare, navigate and share information. Other LAP features include the following:

- LAP upsets and challenges the traditional view that the school language and home languages should be kept separate.
- LAP makes the invisible, visible.
- LAP teaches children to love languages.
- LAP strongly believes that bilinguals use their entire linguistic repertoire to meet their various communicative needs.
- LAP firmly believes that children's learning is enhanced when the new is linked to the known, when new knowledge and experiences are linked to prior knowledge and experiences.
- LAP brings home languages 'out of hiding' (Brown, 2012) and makes them seen, heard, used and included.
- LAP builds on and extends the knowledge, experience, language ability and literacy skills of *all* children.
- LAP serves as a reminder that language and literacy learning exist beyond the classroom.
- LAP enables newcomers to move from a passive place in the classroom to a place where they actively engage and participate.
- LAP enriches, extends and enhances ongoing curriculum and engages *all* children.

More information about LAP

Additional information about LAP can be found in LAP12. In this book you will find discussions about the following topics:

- dynamic bilingualism;
- translanguaging;
- principles of childhood bilingualism;
- importance of children's home languages;
- understanding the dual-language lives of newcomer children;
- transitioning newcomer children from home to classroom;
- partnering with families;
- using home languages in the classroom; and
- documenting classroom language and literacy behaviours.

You will also find discussions about different practices used currently with newcomers and over 50 activities to help you transform your classroom into a multilingual environment.

Multilingual. The term 'multilingual' is used to refer to the presence and use of many languages for communicating, interacting, learning, reading and writing.

School. I use the word 'school' in a broad sense to refer to learning contexts such as childcare centres, preschool groups and classrooms.

School language. This is the language used in the delivery of an education programme. In most cases, the school language is the same as the societal language or the official language (or languages) of a country. For example, in Canada two languages are used in public schools: English and French. In Luxembourg there are three school languages: Luxembourgish, German and French.

Teachers. I use this term broadly to include professionals who work directly and indirectly with children and are responsible for some or all aspects of programme planning, development, delivery and organization. These include childcare staff, kindergarten and primary and junior level teachers, school librarians, speech and language pathologists, settlement workers and school principals.

Theories that Support LAP

 What does it mean to say that LAP is supported by theory?

The simple tree will help answer this question.

According to Thomas Perry, an American arborist,[1] and Peter Wohlleben (2015), a German forester, a tree is an 'integrated phenomenon'. The two main parts – the branches, leaves and trunk above ground and the roots and soil below – work in a two-way (top-to-bottom and bottom-to-top) fashion to ensure healthy growth. For example, injury to one part of the root system will result in the death of the corresponding leaves and branches, or the damage or loss of leaves will result in partial root decline or death.

In the same way, the two parts of the LAP tree (Figure 1.1) – the top or the practice (what?) and the bottom or the theory (why?) – work together. This means that LAP activities and actions are not isolated and stand-alone. Rather, they are supported and explained by teaching and learning theories.

Teachers who are guided by the two parts of the LAP tree are well equipped to create an exciting and challenging learning environment where all children are motivated, engaged and successful. When asked about their instructional practice, these teachers say with confidence: 'This is what I do, and this is why I do it.'

We will look at the visible part of the LAP tree in Chapter 3. The task before us now is to examine the hidden parts of the LAP tree and look at the theories, orientations and frameworks that provide direction to multilingual teaching. The seven theories that support LAP are as follows:

- social justice;
- social constructivism;
- strength-based orientation;
- multiliteracies pedagogy;
- dynamic bilingualism;
- translanguaging; and
- translanguaging practice.

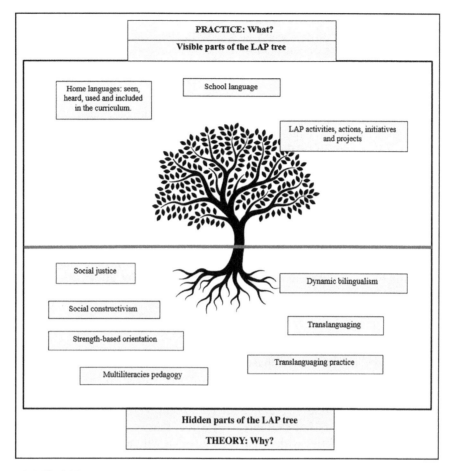

Figure 1.1 The LAP tree

The interested reader will find additional information about the theories in the references provided.

Social justice

Social justice is central to LAP. It promotes tolerance, freedom and equality for every child (García *et al.*, 2017). LAP teachers promote social justice by:

- creating classrooms where *all* children have equal opportunity to participate and learn;
- building on the language, literacy and cultural strengths of *all* children;
- developing an awareness of 'other' language and literacy practices;
- making room for all languages and literacies;

- setting high expectations for *all* children;
- becoming language advocates for *all* children; and
- using valid and fair assessments for *all* children.

Social constructivism

The central idea behind social constructivism is that children construct their knowledge from direct personal experience and from interactions with others. Put forward by Piaget and Vygotsky and elaborated by numerous scholars (Bruner, 1986; Cummins, 2001; Cummins & Early, 2011; Norton, 2000; Piaget, 1929; Siraj-Blatchford & Clarke, 2000; Skourtou *et al.*, 2006; Toohey, 2000; Vygotsky, 1978; Wardle & Cruz-Janzen, 2003), social constructivism describes children's learning as both a personal and a social journey. It positions children as active builders of their own knowledge and emphasizes the importance of social context where their learning is enabled, challenged and supported through interaction with teachers and classmates. The role of the teacher is to support children's learning by providing them with 'high challenge' and 'high-support' and by engaging them in 'rich tasks' (Gibbons, 2009, 2014). We will return to this topic in the next chapter.

Strength-based orientation[2]

LAP is guided by the strength-based orientation (Green *et al.*, 2004). LAP teachers focus on what is 'right' with each child, not what is 'wrong'. They ask the question, 'What is good here?' (Lawrence-Lightfoot & Hoffman Davis, 1997) and look for strengths, skills and abilities in every child. They focus on the whole child and support all areas of development. For example, they know that newcomers are not language novices, but that they arrive with linguistic skills that will help them learn.

LAP teachers encourage all children and families to share their 'funds of knowledge' (Moll *et al.*, 1992) or their cultural, linguistic and professional skills and talents. In this way, they link home and school experiences, tap into children's prior knowledge and provide experiences that are relevant and meaningful for all children.

Multiliteracies pedagogy

Multiliteracies pedagogy was developed in the mid-1990s by the New London Group (Cazden *et al.*, 1996; Cope & Kalantzis, 2000) as a new approach to literacy teaching and learning. It aims to prepare children for a rapidly changing, globalized world. To make teaching and learning more relevant and inclusive, multiliteracies pedagogy focuses on cultural, linguistic, communicative and technological diversity. It calls for the modification of literacy teaching and learning to match the linguistic diversity found in schools, the many new and constantly changing technologies, and the wide range of ways that can be used to represent text.

Multiliteracies pedagogy encourages children to make use of a variety of different formats to create, design and communicate their stories, meanings and experiences. In contrast to traditional teacher-directed literacy pedagogy which focuses on single tools (such as paper and pencils), this rich and engaging approach to literacy allows children to take control of their learning and express their perspectives in their own ways. Multimodal options include paper texts such as books, comics or posters or digital texts such as slide presentations, e-books, e-posters, web pages and film. Multimodal texts can also be live, taking the form of drama, performance, music, singing or spoken language. They can be combined in various ways where a story is told using more than one media platform, all working together to communicate an experience.

Dynamic bilingualism

Early views of bilingualism were built on monolingual ideologies, perspectives and norms (Flores & Schissel, 2014) and described languages as isolated and separate. In contrast to this, dynamic bilingualism (García, 2009a, 2009b, 2009c, 2010) views languages as 'fluid, complex, and dynamic'. This theory focuses on social and communicative aspects of language, such as language practice, actual language use and the languages that bilinguals *use* rather than skills they *have* in separate languages. García defines dynamic bilingualism as 'language practices that are multiple and ever adjusting to the multilingual multimodal terrain of the communicative act'. She reminds us that bilinguals do not separate their two languages. Rather, they translanguage or make use of their entire language repertoire to meet the communicative needs they encounter.

Translanguaging

The term translanguaging refers to a particular way of understanding and describing language and bilingualism. It characterizes bilinguals' language use or *languaging* as fluid and dynamic. It tells us that when bilinguals communicate, they naturally 'shuttle' between their two languages (Canagarajah, 2011). They strategically select words, rules, speaking style and pronunciation (García & Kleyn, 2016) from their *idiolect*, or their unique 'single-competence' or 'one-box' language repertoire which includes features of both of their languages. To navigate and facilitate communication, bilinguals rely on what they know and understand – their cognitive, semiotic, sensory and modal resources. Guided by their *translanguaging instinct*, they adjust language boundaries, disrupt linguistic and cultural cues and move beyond and between language varieties, styles, registers and writing systems (García & Kleyn, 2016; García & Li Wei, 2014; Li Wei, 2016, 2018).

Translanguaging practice

Translanguaging practice (also referred to as translanguaging pedagogy, education and instruction) is a new way of teaching. As school demographics change and classrooms fill with children from different language backgrounds, teachers are adopting this new pedagogy and teaching through a translanguaging lens. Translanguaging practice can be adapted to various educational contexts, levels and programmes. It can be used effectively by monolingual teachers and also by bilingual teachers who do not share the languages of newcomers and bilinguals (García & Sylvan, 2011; García *et al.*, 2016).

Translanguaging practice begins with an understanding of the principles of translanguaging as described above. The next step is to adapt these principles to classroom management and instruction. The goal of translanguaging practice is to build on, extend and sustain the language and literacy practices of all children, help them engage with the curriculum and develop new and meaningful understandings. Two different kinds of classroom translanguaging have been put forward (García & Li Wei, 2014; Lewis *et al.*, 2012). Pupil-directed or natural translanguaging refers to newcomers' free and spontaneous language use, whereas official or teacher-directed translanguaging is the structured multilingual agenda planned and prepared by the teacher. Further, translanguaging practice advocates for translanguaged-mode assessment where bilinguals are given a language choice to display their knowledge and understanding (García & Li Wei, 2014: 134).

Finally, the translanguaging educator views newcomers and bilinguals from two vantage points to help them understand the language demands of each of their two languages. The social view refers to situations with clear language boundaries and rules. In these contexts children are required to inhibit part of their single-language repertoire and use only one of their languages. The second view is individual, where children find themselves in translanguaging spaces, with no language restrictions. In these spaces they can use languages fully, freely and naturally (García & Kleyn, 2016).

Five Reasons to Adopt Multilingual Teaching

'As diversity grows, so must we.'

Howard, 2007

(1) Changing school populations

School populations across Canada, the United States, Australia, the UK, Europe and the Nordic countries are changing and becoming increasingly multilingual and multicultural. These changes are due to the international relocation and displacement of families. A 2016 UNICEF report entitled *Uprooted: The Growing Crisis for Refugee and Migrant Children* shows that nearly 50 million children worldwide have left their homes. Of these, 20 million are migrants who have crossed international borders, 17 million have been internally displaced due to conflict and violence, 10 million are refugees and one million are asylum seekers.

Children from relocated families come from different language, culture and religious groups. Some arrive with their families whereas others are born in the host country. Some are refugees from war-torn countries who have experienced life-changing experiences such as dislocation, change, transition, violence, fear and loss. Some are learning one language at home whereas others are growing up in multiple-language households. Some of these children are literate in their home language whereas others have never been to school or have had their schooling interrupted. These children are faced with the task of navigating their new environments where spaces, places, languages, people, dress, food, weather, behaviours and expectations are unfamiliar and at times daunting.

(2) Shortcomings of monolingual practice

Monolingual practices do not work in linguistically diverse classrooms. Focusing only on the school language does not challenge newcomers or move their learning forward. A classroom driven by the monolingual principle is locked in the local, blocking out the knowledge, skills and enrichment of newcomer children and families. Cummins (2007) urges teachers to acknowledge the linguistic reality of their classrooms, 'free themselves' from monolingual instructional approaches, open their doors to languages and adopt multilingual teaching.

(3) Language as a resource

Following Ruiz (1984), multilingual teaching follows the 'language-as-resource' orientation. This means that LAP teachers view languages as assets. They encourage, nurture and support children's home languages. They draw on and extend newcomers' prior linguistic and cultural knowledge and help them grow bilingually.

(4) Multilingual teaching works!

The many success stories reported in the multilingual literature have made this inclusive practice the 'go to' pedagogy of the 21st century. Reports of excited, engaged and motivated newcomers continue to encourage teachers to embrace this pedagogy and transform their classrooms into multilingual environments.

In the LAP profiles (Chapter 3) you will read about the power of multilingual teaching. You will see how this pedagogy transformed linguistically diverse classrooms and programmes into 'more inhabitable, more equitable, and more efficiently organized spaces for teaching and learning' (Van Avermaet et al., 2018: 1–2).

A recent volume entitled The Multilingual Edge of Education (Van Avermaet et al., 2018) reports on multilingual studies carried out in diverse urban education contexts in Europe, Canada, the USA, Southern Africa and French Guyana. The findings of the reported studies clearly show how 'valorizing' home languages and using them strategically in the classroom and in the curriculum provides newcomers with opportunity and advantage. Here are two examples.

In the action research study reported by Slembrouck et al. (2018), kindergarten and primary grade Turkish-speaking children participated in Turkish language reading and writing activities over a four-year period. The authors report the following qualitative gains for the participants of the study:

- increased self-confidence;
- greater interest in classroom activities and events;
- improved relations with teachers;
- willingness to use the home language in the classroom;
- enhanced language awareness;
- new confidence to speak up in class;
- willingness to collaborate with classmates;
- new interest in reading;
- increased motivation to read in the home language; and
- improved interactions with peers.

Another powerful example of multilingual teaching comes from Nicole, an English as a second language teacher working in a linguistically diverse elementary school in New York (García *et al.*, 2018: 41). The outcome of Nicole's dual-language reading activity showed her the value of including home languages in the curriculum and encouraging newcomers to translanguage to help them be their 'authentic selves' (García *et al.*, 2018: 50). Working with newly arrived Karen[3] speakers, Nicole used *Aesop's Fables*[4] to engage the children in English and Karen literacy activities. Nicole uses three words to describe the response of the children to the dual-language activity: motivated, engaged and attentive (García *et al.*, 2018: 48–49).

(5) Multilingual teaching puts the brakes on children's language loss

By encouraging and supporting home languages, multilingual teaching plays a role in averting or slowing down children's language loss. In classrooms filled with languages, newcomer and bilingual children take pride in their home languages. When they see that their languages are affirmed, encouraged and included, they have a reason to continue learning them.

Consider this …

(1) How has the population of your school changed in the past five years? What is your personal response to these changes?
(2) Recall Howard's (2007) mantra: *'As diversity grows - so must we.'* What does this mean to you as a teacher?
(3) Divide the children in your class into three groups: monolinguals, bilinguals and newcomers.
(4) What does it mean to move the curriculum from the local to the global?
(5) How would you answer this question: 'Why are you/do you want to become a LAP teacher?'

Notes

(1) An arborist is a professional who is trained in the art and science of planting, caring for and maintaining trees and other woody plants. Also see http://arnoldia.arboretum.harvard.edu/pdf/articles/1989-49-4-tree-roots-facts-and-fallacies.pdf.
(2) See http://www.education.vic.gov.au/documents/childhood/professionals/learning/strengthbappr.pdf.
(3) An ethnic group from Burma who are speakers of Karen, a Sino-Tibetan language.
(4) This is a collection of tales from the Greek storyteller, Aesop, who was a keen observer of both animals and people. Most of the characters in the stories are animals, some of which take on human characteristics. Each fable has an accompanying moral to be learned from the tale.

References

Brown, K.D. (2012) The linguistic landscape of educational spaces: Language revitalization and schools in southeastern Estonia. In D. Gorter (ed.) *Minority Languages in the Linguistic Landscape* (pp. 281–298). Basingstoke: Palgrave Macmillan.

Bruner, J.S. (1986) *Actual Minds, Possible Worlds.* Cambridge, MA: Harvard University Press.

Canagarajah, S. (2011) Codemeshing in academic writing: Identifying teachable strategies of translanguaging. *Modern Language Journal* 95, 401–417.

Cazden, C., Cope, B., Fairclough, N., *et al.* (1996) A pedagogy of multiliteracies: Designing social futures. *Harvard Educational Review* 66 (1), 60–86.

Cope, B. and Kalantzis, M. (2000) *Multiliteracies: Literacy Learning and the Design of Social Futures.* London: Routledge.

Cummins, J. (2001) *Negotiating Identities: Education for Empowerment in a Diverse Society* (2nd edn). Los Angeles, CA: California Association for Bilingual Education.

Cummins, J. (2007) Rethinking monolingual instructional strategies in multilingual classrooms. *Canadian Journal of Applied Linguistics* 10 (2), 221–240.

Cummins, J. and Early, M. (eds) (2011) *Identity Texts: The Collaborative Creation of Power in Multilingual Schools.* Stoke-on-Trent: Trentham Books.

Cummins, J. and Persad, R. (2014) Teaching through a multilingual lens: The evolution of EAL policy and practice in Canada. *Education Matters* 2, 3–40.

Flores, N. and Schissel, J.L. (2014) Dynamic bilingualism as the norm: Envisioning a heteroglossic approach to standards-based reform. *TESOL Quarterly* 48 (3), 454–479.

Gallagher, E. (2008) *Equal Rights to the Curriculum: Many Languages, One Message.* Clevedon: Multilingual Matters.

García, O. (2009a) Education, multilingualism and translanguaging in the 21st century. In T. Skutnabb-Kangas, M. Panda and R. Phillipson (eds) *Multicultural Education for Social Justice: Globalizing the Local* (pp. 140–158). New Delhi: Orient Blackswan/Bristol: Multilingual Matters.

García, O. (2009b) *Bilingual Education in the 21st Century: A Global Perspective.* Malden, MA/Oxford: Basil Blackwell.

García, O. (2009c) Emergent bilinguals and TESOL: What's in a name? *TESOL Quarterly* 43 (2), 322–326.

García, O. (2010) Latino language practices and literacy education in the US. In M. Farr, L. Seloni and J. Song (eds) *Ethnolinguistic Diversity and Education: Language, Literacy, and Culture* (pp. 193–211). New York: Routledge.

García, O. and Kleyn, T. (eds) (2016) *Translanguaging with Multilingual Students: Learning from Classroom Moments.* New York: Routledge.

García, O. and Li Wei (2014) *Translanguaging: Language Bilingualism and Education.* New York: Palgrave Macmillan.

García, O. and Sylvan, C. (2011) Pedagogies and practices in multilingual classrooms: Singularities in pluralities. *Modern Language Journal* 95 (iii), 385–400.

García, O., Kleifgen, J.A. and Falchi, L. (2008) *From English Language Learners to Emergent Bilinguals.* Equity Matters Research Review No. 1. New York: Teachers College, Columbia University.

García, O., Ibarra Johnson, S. and Seltzer, K. (2016) *The Translanguaging Classroom: Leveraging Student Bilingualism for Learning.* Philadelphia, PA: Caslon.

García, O., Flores, N. and Spotti, M. (eds) (2017) *The Handbook of Language and Society.* New York/Oxford: Oxford University Press.

García, O., Seltzer, K. and Witt, D. (2018) Disrupting linguistic inequities in US urban classrooms: The role of translanguaging. In P. Van Avermaet, S. Slembrouck, K. Van Gorp, S. Sierens and K. Maryns (eds) *The Multilingual Edge of Education* (pp. 41–66). London: Palgrave Macmillan.

Gibbons, P. (2009) *English Learners, Academic Literacy, and Thinking: Learning in the Challenge Zone.* Portsmouth, NH: Heinemann.

Gibbons, P. (2014) *Scaffolding Language, Scaffolding Learning: Teaching English Language Learners in the Mainstream Classroom.* Portsmouth, NH: Heinemann.

Green, B.L., McAllister, C.I. and Tarte, J.M. (2004) The strengths-based practices inventory: A tool for measuring strengths-based service delivery in early childhood and family support programs. *Families in Society* 85 (3), 327–334.

Howard, G.R. (2007) Responding to changing demographics: As diversity grows, so must we. *Educational Leadership* 64 (6), 16–22.

Lawrence-Lightfoot, S. and Hoffman Davis, J. (1997) *The Art and Science of Portraiture.* San Francisco, CA: Jossey-Bass.

Lewis, G., Jones, B. and Baker, C. (2012) Translanguaging: Developing its conceptualisation and contextualisation. *Educational Research and Evaluation: An International Journal on Theory and Practice* 18 (7), 655–670.

Li Wei (2016) Multi-competence and the translanguaging instinct. In V. Cook and Li Wei (eds) *The Cambridge Handbook of Multi-Competence* (pp. 533–543). Cambridge: Cambridge University Press.

Li Wei (2018) Translanguaging as a practical theory of language. *Applied Linguistics* 39 (1), 9–30.

Moll, L.C., Amanti, C., Neff, D. and González, N. (1992) Funds of knowledge for teaching: Using a qualitative approach to connect homes and classrooms. *Theory into Practice* 31 (2), 132–141.

Norton, B. (2000) *Identity and Language Learning: Gender, Ethnicity and Educational Change.* Harlow: Longman/Pearson Education.

Piaget, J. (1929) *The Child's Conception of the World.* London: Routledge.

Ruiz, R. (1984) Orientations in language planning. *Journal of the National Association for Bilingual Education* 8 (2), 15–34.

Salazar, M. (2013) A humanizing pedagogy: Reinventing the principles and practices of education as a journey toward liberation. *Review of Research in Education* 36 (1), 121–148.

Siraj-Blatchford, I. and Clarke, P. (2000) *Supporting Identity, Diversity and Language in the Early Years.* Philadelphia, PA: Open University Press.

Skourtou, E., Kourtis Kazoullis, V. and Cummins, J. (2006) Designing virtual learning environments for academic language development. In J. Weiss, J. Nolan and P. Trifonas (eds) *International Handbook of Virtual Learning Environments.* Norwell, MA: Springer.

Slembrouck, S., Van Avermaet, P. and Van Gorp, K. (2018) Strategies of multilingualism in education for minority children. In P. Van Avermaet, S. Slembrouck, K. Van Gorp, S. Sierens and K. Maryns (eds) *The Multilingual Edge of Education* (pp. 9–39). London: Palgrave Macmillan.

Toohey, K. (2000) *Learning English in School: Identity, Social Relations and Classroom Practice.* Clevedon: Multilingual Matters.

UNICEF (2016) *Uprooted: The Growing Crisis for Refugee and Migrant Children.* See https://www.unicef.org/publications/index_92710.html (accessed 21 February 2018).

Van Avermaet, P., Slembrouck, S., Van Gorp, K., Sierens, S. and Maryns, K. (2018) *The Multilingual Edge of Education.* London: Palgrave Macmillan.

Vygotsky, L.S. (1978) *Mind in Society: The Development of Higher Social Processes.* Cambridge, MA: Harvard University Press.

Wardle, F. and Cruz-Janzen, M. (2003) *Meeting the Needs of Multiethnic and Multiracial Children in Schools.* Boston, MA: Pearson Education.

Wohlleben, P. (2015) *Hidden Lives of Trees: What They Feel, How They Communicate – Discoveries from a Secret World.* Vancouver: Greystone Books.

2   LAP Teachers

LAP teachers are committed and knowledgeable. Guided by Vygotsky's (1978) theory of social constructivism, they support, facilitate and guide children's learning. Aware of children's different learning needs, LAP teachers bring newcomers, bilinguals and monolinguals together. They provide all children with meaningful tasks, encourage collaboration and, with the help of technological resources, create inclusive and exciting environments where all children can succeed and take control of their learning.

LAP teachers:

- are language activists and language advocates;
- view their classrooms as linguistically complex ecosystems;
- reject the 'silent period';
- understand the learning agenda of all children; and
- rely on technology.

Let's look more closely at these five characteristics of LAP teachers.

(1) LAP Teachers Are Language Activists and Language Advocates

LAP teachers are language activists and language advocates. Their task is bigger than bringing 'as many languages as possible into the curriculum'. According to Christine Hélot (2012), a teacher educator from Strasbourg, France, multilingual teachers have a special relationship with language and languages. They are aware of the rights of children who do not speak the school language. They acknowledge the importance of learning through the home language and recognize that many of the world's languages are threatened and endangered.

LAP teachers are professionally curious and engaged, keeping up to date on multilingual initiatives, developments and resources. They promote and support languages and literacies in their classrooms, share their work with colleagues and partner with families. Many LAP teachers prepare multilingual resources and take an active role in professional activities such as multilingual conferences, workshops, lectures and book clubs.

(2) LAP Teachers View their Classrooms as Linguistically Complex Ecosystems

The term 'linguistically complex ecosystem' comes from the work of two British scholars of bilingualism, Angela Creese and Peter Martin (2006). These two researchers encourage teachers to look at their classrooms as diverse and intricate language networks where languages live, develop, grow, interconnect and interact. With this in mind, LAP teachers nurture the relationships that exist between children, their home languages, the school language and the curriculum.

(3) Silence Is Not Golden: LAP Teachers Reject the 'Silent Period'

Most teachers, early childhood practitioners, language researchers, policymakers, early learning organizations and curriculum writers believe that young newcomers go through a silent period, a quiet and hushed, non-speaking time to 'take in' the school language.

LAP teachers challenge the idea of silent newcomers

LAP teachers are concerned about this thinking and are troubled to see newcomers boxed into a stage and expected to remain silent. They know that the silent period is incompatible with the open and inclusive philosophy of LAP, where children's voices are encouraged and shared, not separated and silenced. They also know that children engaged in learning and enquiry are busy and noisy, not silent. And so LAP teachers question and challenge the silent period.

In order to understand the silent period, we begin with some definitions. We then position newcomers' 'silence' in the wider instructional practice picture, explore its origins, and review recent studies that investigated this 'silent' time in children's second language learning.

 What is the silent period?

Wikipedia defines the silent period as follows: '... a stage in *second language acquisition* where learners do not attempt to speak.'

The silent period, then, is the name given to an early stage in the learning of a new language. Reportedly, it can last weeks, months or even years. The silent period has been defined as the 'absence of speech', a 'solitary space' between the newcomer child's languages and 'a span of time of varying length, during which some beginning second language learners do not willingly produce the language they are learning' (Granger, 2004). Other terms used to describe this period include non-verbal, preproduction, receptive, adjustment, reduced output, transitional and survival. When single words in the new language appear, the silent period comes to an end, and newcomers move on to 'early production', the next stage of their language learning.

The silent period in instructional practice with newcomers

The idea of a silent period has become an established part of teachers' philosophy and practice. Reference to this non-verbal time in children's second language learning can be found across a wide range of education and language resources: in textbooks, professional publications, journal articles, policy and curriculum documents and websites. Described as 'important' and 'beneficial', it has been reported that during the silent period, children engage in the following behaviours:

- take on the role of observer, bystander and onlooker;
- respond 'physically' to happenings in the classroom;
- listen to the new language;
- join in group chants;
- develop a 'readiness' to use the new language;
- collect information about the new language;
- build a vocabulary in the new language;
- experiment with new speech sounds;
- memorize class routines and patterns;
- imitate and mimic classmates;
- communicate non-verbally using facial expressions, vocalizations, body language and gestures;
- repeat formulaic expressions such as 'OK', 'come here', 'go away'; and
- attempt to copy words in the new language from charts and boards.

In current instructional practice, the silent period is both accepted by teachers and expected of newcomers. Teachers view silence as a regular feature of adjustment and language learning. They 'respect' the silent period, expect little from newcomers, give them as much 'quiet' time as they need and bring them into the curriculum only when they have some mastery of the school language. Here are five 'silence' comments from teachers:

'It's only natural that they can't do or say much.'
'They have to listen and observe carefully.'
'It's an important time to quietly crack the code.'
'They have to privately practise, repeat, and experiment with the school language.'
'They should not be forced to speak until they are ready.'

In childcare centres and classrooms, newcomers are automatically assigned to the silent period and expected to begin their language learning in silence. Here are some 'silent period' strategies that have been adopted with newcomers:

- adopt a 'do little' policy;
- accept as fact that children's new language learning is a silent, personal and solitary journey;
- expose children to large amounts of the new language;
- do not hurry children into the new language;
- do not ask them to use the new language;
- believe that newcomers will figure it out and acquire it on their own;
- believe that newcomers are like 'sponges' and will simply soak up the new language; and
- encourage newcomers to demonstrate their understanding through physical actions.

 ## Where does the silent period come from?

The idea of a silent period goes back about 50 years. It emerged between the 1970s and 1980s from research evidence in four disciplines: human learning and development, linguistics, stage theory and second language teaching (Roberts, 2014).

Years ago, developmental scholars, linguists and second language teaching researchers were guided by cognitivism, a theory that emphasized the importance of internal or inborn mechanisms in first language acquisition. From this theory, they made the claim that children learning second languages go through a 'second-language silence' (Roberts, 2014: 33) where they quietly, on their own, figure out the rules of syntax or the grammar of their new language. Only then are they ready to actually use their new language.

Remain silent, understand – and then talk!

Along with this view of children's second language learning came the input hypothesis (Krashen, 1982, 1985), which promised a new way to teach language. This hypothesis put silence on the language learning map and made it a 'feature' of second language learning. According to Roberts, it 'laid the foundation for an assumption of its beneficial nature' (Roberts, 2014: 37). The input hypothesis was initially used with adult learners and was only applied later to young children's language learning. It emphasized the importance of exposure to large amounts of challenging 'comprehensible' language. It claimed that using the new language is not a priority, that it need not be taught or practised: it will simply emerge as the language learner gains competence.

Following this thinking, children's early attempts to use their new language, such as repetitions, imitations, private speech, single-word responses, singing and retelling, were not considered productive language use. Rather, they were viewed as silent behaviours because, the thinking went, they were not creative and lacked an understanding of syntax.

Silence as a stage

During the 1970s and 1980s, when the silent stage was 'most vigorously studied' (Roberts, 2014: 37), the stage model framework, or the consistent ordering of behaviours, was popular among developmental scholars. Fuelled by Piaget's stages of cognitive development and the application of the stage model to first language acquisition, a stage framework for young children's second language learning was developed and the silent period was given a place in this language learning sequence.

In some frameworks the silent period appears as the first stage in children's second language learning, whereas in others it is positioned as Stage 2, following children's fruitless attempts to use their home languages in the classroom.

The four-stage sequence of children's second language learning was promoted and popularized by Tabors (1997) 20 years ago. It set out the 'typical progression' that newcomers follow, from 'persistent silence' to 'repeating words' to 'beginning the process of practicing words and phrases quietly and non-communicatively', and finally 'going public' with the new language. Over the years, this language behaviour sequence solidified silence as a language learning stage and influenced teachers and policy and curriculum writers. To this day, it continues to dominate thinking and writing about first steps in children's additional language learning.

 ## What does research say about the silent period?

Between the 1970s when the silent period was first studied, and the late 1990s when silence was established as a stage in children's second language learning, research interest in this topic was negligible. Since 2000, however, five studies have addressed the silent period in children's second language learning. All five authors agree that newcomers' silence remains 'under-examined' and that there is a 'pressing' need for accurate and systematic investigation of the silent period.

The authors of four of these studies unquestionably accept the idea that newcomer children start their second language learning in silence. They cite the findings of the early silent period studies to justify and explain the silent period. Three of the authors suggest new ways of studying, characterizing and interpreting the silent period, and one cautions against confusing the silent period with an anxiety disorder.

The fifth study differs significantly from the others in that the author does *not* accept the idea of the silent period. Rather, in her in-depth investigation, she questions its widespread acceptance and popularity, documents its origins and critiques the early studies. She raises a red flag and cautions professionals against using outdated and problematic findings as the basis for establishing silence as a stage in young children's second language learning and for making recommendations in early learning policy and curricula.

Let's have a closer look at these studies, starting with the four that accept the silent period as a fact of newcomers' second language learning.

The silent period: A time of 'active interaction'

Sieglová (2011) accepts the idea of newcomer children's silent period and believes that investigations of this topic should be distanced from the traditional language development interpretation. She examines children's silence in social-interactive terms and adopts the communicative analysis approach where attention is on the 'fine interactional detail' of silent behaviours (Sieglová, 2011: 49). She challenges the traditional characterization of silence as passive, uncreative, routine and imitative. Rather, she calls the silence of newcomers 'a social act within talk-in-interaction' (Sieglová, 2011: 58) which includes the sharing and negotiation of meaning.

Newcomers learn through 'silent participation'

Like Sieglová, Bligh (2014) accepts the silent period as a fixed and permanent part of newcomer children's second language journey. In her uneven documentation and at times inaccurate explanations of children's silent behaviours, she reports that during this 'normal' and 'distinct' stage (which can last from six months to over one year) a great deal of 'silent bilingual learning' happens. For example, children actively participate, form their identities and negotiate meanings, all without speaking. In her attempt to 'unpack, analyze and interpret' (Bligh, 2014: 43) the nonverbal experiences and behaviours of 'silent bilingual children', she adopts the sociocultural approach and claims that an understanding of the social and cultural worlds of newcomers will provide teachers with important information about their 'silent experiences', their 'low-power' classroom behaviours (Bligh, 2014: 7) and the nature of second language learning.

The silent period is a journey of language learning and identity formation

Granger's (2004) work centres on educational silence. Like Sieglová and Bligh, she accepts the idea of the silent period as a 'significant aspect' or component of second language acquisition. She views the silent period as a time of language and identity discovery, growth and learning – where silent newcomers engage in learning a new language and form and reform their identities. As they 'dwell … in a solitary space between a first and a second language' (Granger, 2004: 2), she reports that newcomers go through a subjective experience, moving from one language to another and from one self to another one. For Granger, silence serves as an important balance strategy for newcomers who find themselves on 'uncertain ground', suspended 'unsteadily' (Granger, 2004: 78) between two languages, yet 'living fully in neither'. Silence, then is one response to 'a complicated inside and an incomprehensible outside' (Granger, 2004: 77).

The silent period should not be confused with selective mutism

Based on population studies of five countries (USA, Israel, Canada, Switzerland and Germany), Toppelberg *et al.* (2005) report that newcomers or 'immigrant and language minority children' are at a high risk of selective mutism (SM), a type of anxiety disorder characterized by the 'the failure to speak in at least one setting while speaking normally in others'. In their exploration of the relationship between the 'adaptive' silent period and SM, the authors explain that the silent behaviours in both cases make it difficult to distinguish between a 'developmentally typical silent period' and an SM disorder. However, they report that SM *can* be 'suspected' when newcomers exhibit the following four behaviours: silence in both the home and school languages; severe and prolonged silence; limited or no progress; and evidence of shy, anxious or inhibited behaviour.

Challenging the silent period

Unlike the four studies summarized above, Roberts (2014) challenges the idea of a normative silent period and puts forward two never before asked questions about young children's second language learning and teaching:

(1) How did an idea with limited research support come to be accepted, spread and embraced by scholars, early childhood practitioners, policy makers and organizations?
(2) Why does the idea of the silent period continue to dominate and influence second language practice with young newcomers?

To answer these questions, Roberts provides a historical and theoretical explanation of the silent period, and reviews and evaluates 12 silent period studies conducted from the 1970s to the 1990s.

 What did Roberts discover?

Roberts found that research support for the existence of a silent period is 'extremely limited' (Roberts, 2014: 32). She identifies the following shortcomings and flaws in the early studies and calls them 'problematic':

- definitions and explanations of the silent period are either omitted or vary across studies;
- the meaning of silence and its relationship to measured language acquisition is unexplained;
- key constructs are oversimplified and overgeneralized;
- theories put forward to support the existence of the silent period are not clear;
- stage/phase/period theory explanations are not provided;
- demographic and contextual data is incomplete; and
- conclusions are often assertions made by the authors.

 What does Roberts conclude?

Roberts concludes the following about the silent period:

- The extent and quality of the research evidence for a silent period in childhood second language acquisition is 'extremely limited'.
- The findings of the silent period studies should not be generalized.

- The findings of the 12 studies should *not* be used as a basis for recommendations for position statements, policies and instructional practice.
- The participants in the studies (mostly high socio-economic status) are not representative of newcomers in classrooms today.
- Calling the silent period a 'typical feature' of childhood second language acquisition is inaccurate.
- The acceptance of the silent period is unsubstantiated, unconfirmed and doubtful.
- The need for an accurate understanding of the silent period is 'pressing'.
- Acceptance of the silent period as a feature of second language learning has significant consequences for language development.

Let's go back and respond to the two questions that guided Robert's work on the silent period.

(1) How did an idea with limited research support come to be accepted, spread and embraced by scholars, early childhood practitioners, policy makers and organizations?

The idea of the silent period was born a long time ago, in the 1970s and 1980s. It emerged from shifts, developments and changes found in four research disciplines: human learning and development, linguistics, stage theory and second language teaching. Stated differently, the idea of a silent, passive time for young children learning a second language came about because of the focus on internal mechanisms in language learning and the belief that large amounts of language input will result in language use and the sequential ordering of language behaviours.

(2) Why does the idea of the silent period continue to dominate and influence second language practice with young newcomers to this day?

The answer to this question is straight forward. The idea of the silent period as a distinct stage in children's second language learning has, in the past 30 years, taken on myth status. Lack of interest and understanding, have allowed the idea of children's silence to morph into a tradition that remains accepted, expected and unquestioned to this day.

Summary

To summarize what we have learned about the silent period, let's do two things:

- separate silent period myths from facts (Table 2.1); and
- take a firm stand on the silent period.

LAP teachers take a stand on the silent period

Guided by the work of Roberts, LAP teachers take a firm stand on the silent period by:

- rejecting the idea of a silent period in newcomers' language learning;
- considering it both harmful and discriminatory; and
- asserting that it is the monolingual agenda that *silences* newcomers.

Table 2.1 The silent period: Separating myths from facts

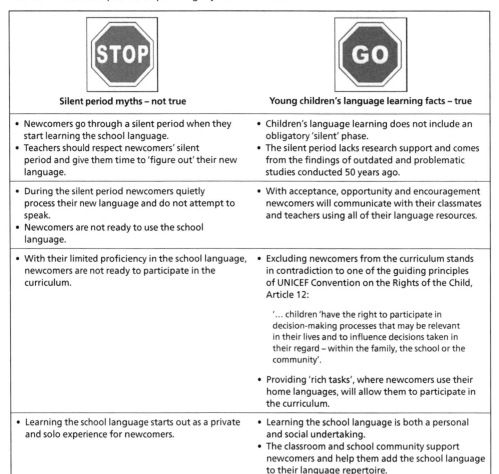

Silent period myths – not true	Young children's language learning facts – true
• Newcomers go through a silent period when they start learning the school language. • Teachers should respect newcomers' silent period and give them time to 'figure out' their new language.	• Children's language learning does not include an obligatory 'silent' phase. • The silent period lacks research support and comes from the findings of outdated and problematic studies conducted 50 years ago.
• During the silent period newcomers quietly process their new language and do not attempt to speak. • Newcomers are not ready to use the school language.	• With acceptance, opportunity and encouragement newcomers will communicate with their classmates and teachers using all of their language resources.
• With their limited proficiency in the school language, newcomers are not ready to participate in the curriculum.	• Excluding newcomers from the curriculum stands in contradiction to one of the guiding principles of UNICEF Convention on the Rights of the Child, Article 12: '… children 'have the right to participate in decision-making processes that may be relevant in their lives and to influence decisions taken in their regard – within the family, the school or the community'. • Providing 'rich tasks', where newcomers use their home languages, will allow them to participate in the curriculum.
• Learning the school language starts out as a private and solo experience for newcomers.	• Learning the school language is both a personal and social undertaking. • The classroom and school community support newcomers and help them add the school language to their language repertoire.

(4) LAP Teachers Understand the Learning Agendas of *All* Children

LAP teachers are tuned in to children's needs. They understand that the learning demands or learning agendas of monolingual, bilingual and newcomer children are not the same.

For example, they know that the classroom and the school are familiar and predictable places for children who speak the school language. They also know that bilingual children walk in two language worlds and that newcomers face numerous challenges when they join classrooms where everything happens in a language they do not understand.

Matt, Alvaro and Hawra

To better understand this, let's look at the learning agendas of three children. Seven-year-old Matt, Alvaro and Hawra are in the same Grade 2 class in Maple Public School, an English-medium school located in a large Canadian city.

- **Matt** is a monolingual speaker of English. He has been in Maple Public School since kindergarten. Matt is an outgoing child and has many friends. Matt actively participates in the curriculum. He loves numbers and happily engages in numeracy activities.
- **Alvaro** is a Portuguese-English bilingual. He arrived in the Maple Public School kindergarten four years ago as a newcomer, speaking only Portuguese. Alvaro is now a speaker of English, which is his stronger language. His home language is Portuguese and he attends Portuguese language classes on Saturday mornings. Alvaro loves soccer and works well with his classmates.
- **Hawra** is an Arabic-speaking newcomer. Her arrival in Maple Public School upset her personally, emotionally, socially, linguistically and academically. Faced with a new language and an unfamiliar classroom, she questions who she is and what she knows. She observes her surroundings, listens carefully, and tries to fit in, make friends and join in with the life of the classroom. When invited to participate in the curriculum, she is cautious and hesitant. With very little English, she feels unsure and incapable.

The learning agendas of Matt, Alvaro and Hawra are illustrated in Table 2.2. Column A shows the developmental and curricular requirements for all three children. Column B shows Alvaro and Hawra's extra learning tasks. In addition to the learning requirements listed in Column A, these two children are faced with additional learning on many levels.

 ### How does the LAP teacher support children's learning agendas?

LAP teachers provide all children with 'rich tasks' (Gibbons, 2009, 2014). These relevant and meaningful activities allow children to work together, tap into their prior knowledge and use all their linguistic and literacy resources. Rich tasks are especially important for newcomers. In contrast to the 'busy' activities they are often given, such as worksheets and copying, rich tasks bring newcomers into the curriculum, encourage them to connect with classmates, help them learn the school language in meaningful contexts and give them a sense of purpose and belonging.

'Our languages': An example of a rich task

In this task, Matt, Alvaro and Hawra set out on a language fact-finding mission. The purpose was to gain an understanding of one another's language. Working together, they

Table 2.2 Learning agendas: Monolingual Matt, bilingual Alvaro and newcomer Hawra

(A) Learning agenda: Matt, Alvaro and Hawra	(B) Additional learning agenda: bilingual Alvaro; newcomer Hawra
Personal • identity • home experiences • life experiences • dress • food • behaviours • culture • religion	• walking in two language worlds • navigating new layers of identity • finding their place and voice in the new school • using prior learning • continued use of the home language • adding a new language • participating in home language community events
Language • continued development of English • learning academic English	
Social • interactions • relationships • friendships • school and majority culture	
Academic (cognitive) • Grade 2 curriculum	

talked about English, Portuguese and Arabic. They visited language sites and gathered facts about their languages, prepared a presentation and shared it with the class.

Matt: English

Matt used a world map to show the many countries where English is spoken. He shared an important fact that gave all of his classmates, especially the monolinguals, a sense of pride: English is a global language with 1.5–2 billion speakers worldwide. Matt created a word list that included terms such as 'pronunciation', 'accent' and 'dialect' to explain language variation. When he shared YouTube clips of the varieties of English, his classmates were captivated and attempted words and phrases in different English accents.

Alvaro: Portuguese

In his presentation, Alvaro shared facts about the Portuguese language. Of interest to his Arabic-speaking classmates was the Arabic origin of some Portuguese words. This engaged Hawra and other Arabic-speaking children. They worked together to find these words and created a Portuguese-Arabic-English word list which included 'sugar', 'olive oil', 'village' and the term 'God willing'.

Hawra: Arabic

Hawra used a chart (Figure 2.1) to explain the Arabic writing system. With her limited command of English, she presented in Arabic while her classmate (the child to

Figure 2.1 Hawra presenting the Arabic writing system

her left) provided simultaneous English interpretation. Hawra's classmates were especially interested in two main differences between Arabic and English: the number of letters in the alphabet (Arabic has 28, English has 26) and text directionality (Arabic follows right-to-left and English left-to-right).

The role of the LAP teacher during rich tasks

As children engage in rich tasks, LAP teachers provide high support. They move from group to group, monitoring, mediating and facilitating. When necessary, they explicitly teach and provide information. They evaluate and document children's behaviours, performance and progress. To do this, they adopt an interactive technique called dynamic assessment (DA).

 ## What is dynamic assessment?

Grounded in Vygotsky's social constructivism, DA is a highly interactive and flexible tool to support, teach, guide and assess children's skill development and learning potential. DA maintains the connection between learning, teaching and evaluation and is not limited to any one content area or to any specific age or population. DA focuses on the processes of learning, rather than on the static assessment of end products or isolated skills (Lantolf & Poehner, 2004, 2007, 2010; Lidz & Elliott, 2000; Tzureil, 2001). DA helps children understand *how* to do something, not just *what* to do. It also encourages them to transfer learned skills across tasks so that they can work independently. DA is widely used by teachers, psychologists and speech and language pathologists to monitor and evaluate children's abilities in language, maths, reading and general intelligence.

Here are the main features of DA:

- begins with the teacher's understanding of children's learning agendas and needs;
- includes both interaction and intervention;
- embeds instruction in the assessment process;
- emphasizes the learning process;
- scaffolds learning;
- promotes development;
- identifies both individual skills and learning potential;
- measures ability to learn, transfer and modify learning strategies;
- measures children's engagement and response to learning;
- positions children to take control of their learning;
- assesses a variety of content domains;
- encourages self-regulation;
- is flexible in its application and choice of contexts, materials and topics;
- looks at children's reactions to teaching and learning;
- is conducted in several sessions over a relatively brief time period;
- includes flexible interpretations and recommendations;
- is designed and customized by the teacher; and
- informs teaching.

DA in action

To see how DA works, we go back to the language fact-finding task described earlier. As Matt, Alvaro and Hawra collected information about their home languages, Tobin (the LAP teacher) took on the role of 'guide on the side'. He didn't tell the children *what* to do, but helped them understand the task requirements and challenged them to figure out *how* to proceed. In this way, he positioned them to work together and take control of their learning.

For Tobin, the language fact-finding groups were learning zones that rest between how children manage the task on their own and what they can do with his guidance. Tobin interacted with each group several times and provided guidance and support. His strategic questioning and prompts helped the children focus on central ideas, identify challenges and explain their work. When the children showed signs of managing on their own, Tobin stepped back.

On a number of occasions Tobin directly intervened in the fact-finding task. For example, at one point he noticed that Alvaro and Hawra were getting most of the attention, leaving Matt somewhat disengaged. He then introduced the topic of language variation and explained to the children that some languages (including English) are spoken in different ways in different places. Tobin then adopted the 'don't tell' strategy and provided no further information about language variation. Instead, remembering that discovery and collaboration lead to understanding, he invited Matt to take the lead on the English language variation task. When he returned to the group some time later, he asked Matt to explain the steps taken and report on plans for presentation.

(5) LAP Teachers Rely on Technology

In most cases, LAP teachers do not understand or speak the children's home languages. For this reason, they rely on electronic technologies such as small mobile computers, translation apps, portable electronic translators, electronic books and story apps in order to connect with newcomers, integrate them into the classroom and engage them in the curriculum (Parker, 2008).

In the following example, you will read how one group of teachers (Grades 2, 3, 5 and English as a second language) in a Toronto school used technology-mediated activities to welcome, integrate and support a group of Arabic-speaking children newly arrived from Syria.

Getting ready

When the newcomers arrived, the LAP teachers were ready: English-Arabic translation apps were downloaded onto their cell phones; and Arabic-English translation and picture dictionary apps (which included an audio function allowing viewers to scan pages to hear words spoken in both Arabic and English) were downloaded on classroom tablets and computers, as were age-appropriate Arabic and bilingual (Arabic-English) stories. In addition to this, Arabic-English/English-Arabic picture dictionaries were waiting on the classroom library shelf. Also, all speakers of Arabic (children, teachers and school staff) were on standby.

All of the newcomers, even the shy and guarded ones, were excited to try out the tablets and computers. They were encouraged to explore and test the functions and features of the devices. When the Arabic language apps were introduced, some expressed surprise and others laughed and nodded as they tapped, swiped, listened and attempted words and phrases in their new language. They worked alone, in pairs, in a group or with the teacher. They were free to work in the classroom, in the hallway or in the school library.

LAP teachers reported that early interactions with tablets and computers were an important and engaging welcome for newcomer children. They provided an exciting entry into the new classroom, eased separation from parents, created a sense of independence, purpose and belonging and helped them connect with classmates and teachers. Also, exploring the devices helped the newcomers discover the school language.

After a period of exploration and discovery, the children were invited to add Arabic to the blackboard classroom agenda. Working together, they used translation and dictionary apps and Arabic keyboards to prepare a bilingual (English-Arabic) class schedule (Figure 2.2) and labels for classroom items, materials and furniture. These tasks integrated the newcomers into the classroom, helped them navigate their new environment, showed them that their home languages had a place in the classroom, and helped them start learning the school language.

Figure 2.2 English-Arabic class schedule

A three-step activity: Tell me your story

Once the newcomers were familiar with the tablets, computers and keyboards, LAP teachers guided them in a literacy project called 'Tell me your story'. In this three-step task, newcomers used their home language literacy skills to participate in a personalized literacy activity.

Step 1: Getting started

The activity began with a group discussion about home, family, country, language, names, appearance, skin colour, celebrations, food, clothing, dance, faith, music, friends, school, sports, flags and hobbies. Newcomers were invited to share their experiences and talk about things that were important to them. Books and photographs were used to generate and sustain discussion. Teachers used guiding statements and sentence frames such as: *I come from …*; *My name means …*; *My family came to Canada when …*; *When my family lived in …*; and *I really like …*, to keep the discussion flowing. Arabic-speaking classmates served as language buddies and interpreters and encouraged the newcomers to contribute their ideas.

Step 2: Creating identity texts

Following the group discussion, the children worked together to plan, create word lists and organize their ideas into personal life stories or identity texts. They worked with partners or in small groups. They selected their working language or languages (Arabic, Arabic and English, or English), their materials (paint, markers, paper or craft materials), the resources (books and websites), their workplace (classroom or library), the format (music, drama and dance) and the technology tools (story apps, tablet or computer, Arabic keyboard or Arabic-English translator application). The teachers monitored and supported their efforts and encouraged them to create multimodal digital stories using a combination of pictures, sounds, music, diagrams and written text (Figure 2.3).

Step 3: Sharing identity texts

Newcomers shared their identity texts with classmates, with the teacher, with school visitors (Figure 2.4) and also with the principal during his classroom visits. Some

Figure 2.3 Pages from an identity text

Figure 2.4 Sharing identity texts with the author

of the personal stories were posted on the school Dual Language Showcase (http://schools.peelschools.org/1363/DualLanguage/Documents/index.htm). The teachers reported that this 'powerful and heartwarming' sharing presented the identities of the newcomers in a positive light. The encouraging response from teachers ('Good for you', 'Well done') gave newcomers a sense of success, pride and confidence. The enthusiastic reaction of classmates ('Your English is real good', 'Awesome!', 'Great job!') showed them that their stories mattered and that they belonged in their new class.

Taking the identity texts home provided newcomer families with 'personalized windows' into their children's school experiences and helped bridge the home with the school. Parents were encouraged to talk about and extend their children's identity texts and create additional ones.

From identity texts into the curriculum

Creating personal stories or identity texts encouraged newcomers to 'jump' into the curriculum and actively engage in language, maths and science lessons and activities. The now-familiar collaborative approach used to prepare identity texts was used in topic-specific projects and activities. With the help of Arabic-speaking peers, Arabic keyboards and relevant websites and apps, newcomers prepared dual-language projects. For example, Figure 2.5 shows brainstorming in Arabic and English about rewriting a story ending, and in Figure 2.6 the key words of a science lesson (force and motion) are listed in Arabic and in English. Like the personal identity texts, completed projects were presented to the class (in Arabic and in English), displayed in the classroom and often shared with the school principal.

Newcomer children were proud of their collaborative curriculum work. The recognition and success of their first projects showed them that even without full mastery of English, they could participate and contribute in meaningful ways.

Figure 2.5 Bilingual brainstorming

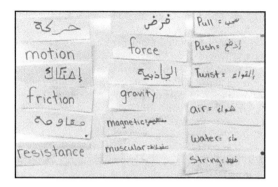

Figure 2.6 Science bilingual word list

Consider this …

(1) Why do LAP teachers reject the idea of a 'silent period'?
(2) Compare the learning agendas of monolinguals, bilinguals and newcomers.
(3) The LAP teacher provides all children with high challenges. What does this mean to you?
(4) How do you use technology to support your multilingual teaching?
(5) Identity texts have been mainly used to integrate newcomers. How can they be used with all children?

References

Bligh, C. (2014) *The Silent Experiences of Young Bilingual Learners: A Sociocultural Study into the Silent Period*. Rotterdam: Sense.

Creese, A. and Martin, P. (2006) Linguistic diversity in the classroom: An ecological perspective. *NALDIC Quarterly* 3 (3), 27–32.

Gibbons, P. (2009) *English Learners, Academic Literacy, and Thinking: Learning in the Challenge Zone*. Portsmouth, NH: Heinemann.

Gibbons, P. (2014) *Scaffolding Language, Scaffolding Learning: Teaching English Language Learners in the Mainstream Classroom*. Portsmouth, NH: Heinemann.

Granger, C.A. (2004) *Silence in Second Language Learning*. Clevedon: Multilingual Matters.

Hélot, C. (2012) Linguistic diversity and education. In M. Martin-Jones, A. Blackledge and A. Creese (eds) *The Routledge Handbook of Multilingualism*. London: Routledge.

Krashen, S.D. (1982) *Principles and Practice in Second Language Acquisition*. Oxford: Pergamon Press.

Krashen, S.D. (1985) *The Input Hypothesis*. Harlow: Longman.

Lantolf, J.P. and Poehner, M.E. (2004) Dynamic assessment: Bringing the past into the future. *Journal of Applied Linguistics* 1, 49–74.

Lantolf, J.P. and Poehner, M.E. (2007) Dynamic assessment. In E. Shohamy and N. Hornberger (eds) *Encyclopedia of Language and Education: Language Testing and Assessment* (pp. 273–285). Berlin: Springer.

Lantolf, J.P. and Poehner, M.E. (2010) Dynamic assessment in the classroom: Vygotskian praxis for second language development. *Language Teaching Research* 15 (1), 11–33.

Lidz, C.S. and Elliott, J.G. (2000) *Dynamic Assessment: Prevailing Models and Applications*. Amsterdam: Elsevier.

Parker, L. (ed.) (2008) *Technology-mediated Learning Environments for Young English Learners: Connections In and Out of School*. New York: Lawrence Erlbaum.

Roberts, T.A. (2014) Not so silent after all: Examination and analysis of the silent stage in childhood second-language acquisition. *Early Childhood Research Quarterly* 29 (4), 22–40.

Sieglová, D. (2011) The role of 'silence' in child second-language interaction: A single-case micro-analysis of a 7-year-old Czech girl's interaction in an English speaking environment. *Journal of Applied Linguistics* 1, 43–64.

Tabors, P.O. (1997) *One Child, Two Languages: A Guide for Preschool Educators of Children Learning English as a Second Language*. Baltimore, MD: Paul H. Brookes.

Toppelberg, C.O., Tabors, P., Coggins, A., Lum, K. and Burger, C. (2005) Differential diagnosis of selective mutism in bilingual children. *Journal of the American Academy of Child and Adolescent Psychiatry* 44, 592–595.

Tzuriel, D. (ed.) (2001) *Dynamic Assessment of Young Children*. Plenum Series on Human Exceptionality. New York: Springer.

UNICEF Conventions on the Rights of the Child. *Factsheet*. See https://www.unicef.org/crc/files/Right-to-Participation.pdf (accessed 10 March 2018).

Vygotsky, L.S. (1978) *Mind in Society: The Development of Higher Social Processes*. Cambridge, MA: Harvard University Press.

Wikipedia (2018) *Silent Period*. See https://en.wikipedia.org/wiki/Silent_period.

3 LAP Profiles: Journeys, Actions, Projects and More …

In the first two chapters, you read about the nuts and bolts of LAP. It is now time to look at LAP 'in action' and see how it plays out in real classrooms, with real children, teachers and families.

The 15 profiles included in this chapter showcase the multilingual teaching experiences of over 50 contributors (teachers-in-training, classroom teachers, special programme teachers, school principals and a language consultant), working in two contexts (schools and specialized programmes) in five countries (Canada, Germany and Luxembourg, Iceland and Sweden). Some of the profiles were prepared using templates, whereas others were written as narratives. Completed profiles were formatted and edited, and are presented in three groups: LAP journeys, LAP in schools and LAP in specialized programmes:

LAP Journeys
(1) Teachers-in-training
(2) Discovery of LAP
(3) Swedish as a second language teacher
(4) Early childhood professional
(5) English as a second language teacher

LAP in Schools
Canada
(1) Beaver Valley team
(2) Halifax schools
(3) Thornwood team

Germany, Iceland, Luxembourg, Sweden
(4) A kindergarten classroom
(5) Icelandic preschools
(6) Luxembourg classrooms
(7) A school in Sweden

LAP in Specialized Programmes
(1) Preschool
(2) Language intervention
(3) English as a second language

In some profiles schools are named, whereas in others pseudonyms are used. The names of the contributors are included in each profile. Their short biographies can be found in the List of Contributors.

Note: Taken together, the 15 LAP profiles represent only a slice of the global multilingual teaching pie … and a big pie it is! It includes teachers who are responding to changes in school populations and adopting multilingual teaching in creative and unique ways. My hope is that the LAP profiles will inspire you to review your current practice and join the global multilingual teaching movement.

Five Reading Tips

5

(1) *Revisit the LAP tree*. Before you read the profiles, go back to the LAP tree (Chapter 1). Remember how LAP was compared to the two parts of a tree? The hidden part of the LAP tree or the theories that support LAP were explained in Chapter 1. Our task now is to explore the visible part of the LAP tree, the practice that includes multilingual activities, actions, journeys, initiatives and projects.
(2) *Discuss and share*. Read the LAP profiles on your own, or do so with your colleagues. Read them in the order in which they are presented, or choose your own order. Add them to your professional book club reading list. Discuss and share the information found in the profiles.
(3) *Home languages in the profiles*. The inclusion of home languages and literacies is key to multilingual teaching. As you read the profiles, pay attention to the presence of home languages (Figure 3.1). Are they seen? Are they heard? Are they used? Are they included in the curriculum?

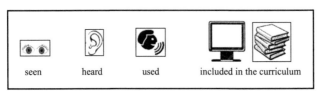

seen   heard   used   included in the curriculum

Figure 3.1 Home languages in the classroom

(4) *Your LAP journey.* As you read the profiles, think about your own multilingual teaching journey. When did you first come across multilingual teaching? What was your initial response? How has your multilingual teaching evolved and changed?

(5) *Which LAP actions are for you?* Which LAP actions included in the profiles do you find most interesting? Could they work in your classroom? What kind of modifications or adjustments would you need to make in order for them to work?

LAP Journeys

(1) Teachers-in-training
(2) Discovery of LAP
(3) Swedish as a second language teacher
(4) Early childhood professional
(5) English as a second language teacher

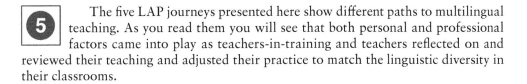 The five LAP journeys presented here show different paths to multilingual teaching. As you read them you will see that both personal and professional factors came into play as teachers-in-training and teachers reflected on and reviewed their teaching and adjusted their practice to match the linguistic diversity in their classrooms.

LAP Journey 1: Teachers-in-training

Jessica Altimari, Paige Badger, Wei Cao Zi, Candice Chan, Lan Chan, Tegan Chan, Jessy Choi, Christina Cinelli, Jessica Cipparrone, Allison Diolanda, Ikram Dirie, Sarah Maggie El'Lithy, Humaira Gharayia, Sharon Hartman, Eunice Joo, Christie Leung, Camila Macdonald, An Mai, Marta Masnij, Adizat Ofulue, Alfie Ogalesco, Lasheka Packkiyarajah, Lubomyr Stasyszyn, Meaghan Sullivan, Iqura Tariq and Zhen Wang Qiao

'It is important to show these children that their home language is valued and special.'

This LAP journey describes the experiences of a group of teachers-in-training who completed a 13-week practicum in a linguistically diverse Ontario school. The students were in a four-year undergraduate programme in early childhood studies at Ryerson University (Toronto, Canada). They were from diverse language backgrounds: two were monolingual speakers of English and the others were bilingual or multilingual speakers of the following 14 languages: Arabic, Cantonese, Gujarati, Hindi, Italian, Japanese, Korean, Mandarin, Somali, Tagalog, Vietnamese, Ukrainian, Urdu and Yoruba.

One month before the start of the practicum, the students met with their faculty advisor for an information seminar. They were introduced to LAP and assigned to their classrooms (kindergarten to Grade 5). Practicum requirements included working closely with field educators to introduce, extend and/or enrich the classroom multilingual agenda. Students were also required to document their experiences in weekly journals.

First impressions, successes, concerns and challenges

In the early weeks, the students described their apprehension and anxiety about three things: (a) joining a new classroom and being accepted and liked by the children; (b) their preparedness to work with children and families from diverse language backgrounds; and (c) communicating with children who speak little or no English. The students were happy to work in pairs and share their very first multilingual teaching experience.

> 'When we first did LAP, the children were not as connected, but as the weeks went by, I noticed that the children were very proud and excited to share their home languages with each other.'

As the students started their multilingual work, they quickly realized that there were limitations and gaps in their understanding of languages, cultures and religions. They noted the following in their journals:

- 'I have become quite aware of how little I know about cultures, languages and religions of the world.'
- 'I feel embarrassed admitting this, but my interactions with the children and teachers in this school have really opened my eyes to how I need to educate myself on different languages, cultures and religions.'

The bilingual students admitted apprehension in sharing their home languages with children:

- 'I don't feel comfortable sharing my Mandarin language and culture with the children.'
- 'I've never used my language in a practicum before.'

Children's unwillingness to use home languages in the classroom

In the first weeks of placement, the students documented their surprise at the children's unwillingness to use their home languages. While interest in LAP activities was high, invitations to use home languages were mostly met with unwillingness, confusion or silence. Especially challenging was working with the newly arrived children who spoke Arabic to everyone.

LAP takes off!

5

As the students extended the multilingual agendas in their classrooms, the children 'warmed up' to the idea of using and sharing their home languages. The unwillingness noted in the early weeks was replaced by excitement, as children engaged in purposeful and spontaneous language inquiry. Here are five behaviours documented in student journals:

(1) More and more children talked about their own language and the languages of classmates and visitors:
   - *'Yeah, I'm bilingual. I know Arabic and English.'*
   - *'His language is Tagalog, right?'*
   - *'Hi, you speak Arabic?'*
   - *'Do you talk like me?'*
(2) Many children offered to help newcomers from Syria:
   - *'I'll help. I know English and I know Arabic.'*
(3) Children sang in their home languages:
   - *'I'm singing a song in Tamil, that's my language. It's a song about a hero riding a horse with a carrot.'*
(4) Translanguaging, or the going back and forth across languages, was evident during activity time:
   - *'There is cloud, snow and shumsa (sun in Arabic).'*
   - *'That me and that's nonno (grandfather in Italian).'*
(5) Children showed interest in home language literacies. For example, they used their bilingual name cards to sign completed work:
   - *'I can make my name three ways: Arabic, Spanish and English. My father is from Saudi Arabia, my mother is Spanish and I am English.'*

From uncertainty to professional growth

The multilingual teaching practicum was a new and exciting experience for the students. Over the 13-week period they journeyed from anxious observers to confident, knowledgeable practitioners. Guided and mentored by seasoned multilingual educators, they witnessed the natural inclusion of home languages in classrooms and participated in the unique experience of integrating newcomers from Syria. These experiences helped them understand the importance of home languages and changed their thinking about instructional practice with newcomers. In their final journal entries, the students described their professional growth and their commitment to multilingual teaching. They left their placement committed to 'teaching through a multilingual lens' (Cummins & Persad, 2014), ready to develop and launch their own multilingual teaching agendas.

LAP Journey 2: Discovery of LAP

Tracy O'Hara

> '... equity, inclusiveness, and being culturally responsive matter to me!'

At the time of writing, Tracy, a monolingual, English speaker, was in the final year of a teacher preparation programme in a Canadian university. Her LAP journey started during an internship with newcomers. She noticed that they were disengaged, quiet, and often responded to her questions with single words. However, when they engaged in 'playful storytelling' (narrating and recording their spontaneous play), they were happy and excited, mixing English with their home languages and using English in ways that 'did not quite make sense to me'. When she tried to support and extend their stories, Tracy found that she was unsure of how best to proceed. Questions flooded her mind and she decided to do something about this 'internal conflict weighing on my heart and mind'.

Tracy portrayed her dilemma in a visual (Figure 3.2), using dark colours to represent her incomplete understanding of language learning, culture, bilingualism and effective practice with newcomers. She then set out to discover what was 'holding newcomers back'.

LAP12 helped Tracy think about English-only classrooms in new ways. She thought about how monolingual focused teaching silences newcomers and how the

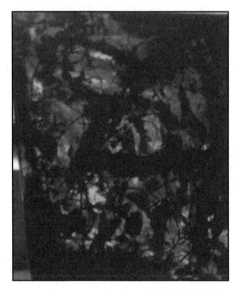

Figure 3.2 Tracy's dilemma

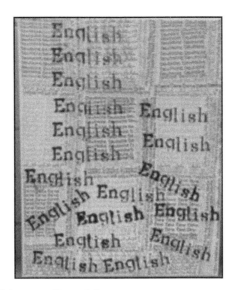

Figure 3.3 Tracy's view of the monolingual class

label 'English language learner' (ELL) fails to capture the potential and the learning of these 'emergent bilinguals'. She saw that in English-only classrooms children's home languages are discounted, English-language assessments are unfair and English is viewed as the superior and preferred language. Her second visual (Figure 3.3) reflects the monolingual English language classroom, a place that 'covers up and overtakes the

Figure 3.4 Tracy's resolve

stories of newcomer children'. In the image, the word ENGLISH is in the forefront with the names of home languages blurred and distant, yet present in the background.

As Tracy's LAP journey continued, she noted that home languages were absent from cultural celebrations and that 'responsiveness' to cultures omitted home languages. Her third and final visual (Figure 3.4) is a testament to her resolve to focus on LAP and advocate for all children. She set out to ensure that all children have the opportunity to 'showcase their strengths, share stories, play, create, and solve problems in classrooms that support multi-language and literacy learning'. To share her experiences with other teachers, Tracy has created a website: https://lap-ece.squarespace.com/.

LAP Journey 3: A Swedish as a Second Language Teacher

Anneli Wessman

'I was curious and asked questions.'

Anneli's personal and professional experiences shaped her LAP journey. As a child, Anneli emigrated with her family from Finland to Sweden. In school, she was forbidden to speak her native Finnish and recalls that teachers had no interest in her language background and abilities. She accepted the shift to Swedish as natural, and over the years lost her Finnish and part of her identity: 'Today I barely can speak Finnish and I lost a big part of my Finnish identity.'

Many years later, as a classroom teacher, Anneli repeated what she had experienced as a child. She adopted both assimilative and supportive practice with the newcomers in her class, convinced that they too would lose their home languages and become monolingual speakers of Swedish.

Yet this practice did not sit well with Anneli. She questioned the effectiveness of her practice with newcomers and realized that she needed to better understand them in order to support their learning. This led her to complete a number of Swedish as a second language (SSL) courses at the University of Stockholm and at the University Dalarna. She learned about second language learning, discovered multilingual pedagogy, engaged in discussions with other teachers and changed her thinking about supporting and teaching newcomer children. Anneli describes her shift to LAP as a gradual process that 'happened slowly' and included reflection, review and study.

Today Anneli is an SSL teacher and a LAP advocate. She works in a highly diverse school in Sweden where 80% of the children are from non-Swedish speaking homes. She continues to be professionally curious, presents her LAP strategies and plans at workshops and conferences, keeps up to date on multilingual resources and research, writes papers and reports and prepares multilingual resources. She describes the diversity in Swedish schools as 'enrichment' for all.

LAP Journey 4: An Early Childhood Professional

Angélique Sanders

'I want to support what the children brought to the classroom.'

Angelique is a dedicated and experienced, multilingual teacher. She has been working for more than 20 years with children aged two to six in a laboratory school housed on a Canadian university campus. Fluent in Dutch (her native language) and English, she also has basic communication skills in French, Spanish, Arabic, Italian and ASL (American Sign Language). Angelique describes languages as her hobby and her passion.

In her early teaching years, Angelique naturally and spontaneously brought her language skills into the classroom. As she helped young newcomers learn English to 'help them fit in', she also used other languages in the classroom. For example, she included Dutch and French songs and stories, taught children basic ASL and used non-English directives to refocus and redirect behaviour. The children's enthusiastic response to hearing unfamiliar languages encouraged Angelique to engage them in developmentally appropriate discussions about the many different ways people talk.

Explanations, ideas and suggestions found in LAP12 matched Angelique's vision for teaching newcomers and she quickly and enthusiastically extended her teaching. By implementing LAP activities, she transformed her classroom into a multilingual space where children explored each other's home languages and literacies and where families participated in the programme, reading books, singing, and sharing their 'funds of knowledge' (Moll *et al.*, 1992). In this multilingual space, children proudly stepped into the role of language teachers, announcing: 'This is how you say it in my language.'

Angelique's commitment to multilingual teaching extends far beyond her classroom. She works closely with her colleagues to ensure centre-wide commitment to LAP, keeps informed about new multilingual events and resources, mentors undergraduate students who are assigned practicum in her classroom and presents her multilingual work at early childhood conferences and workshops. She has also worked as a multilingual teaching coach, supporting and mentoring teachers new to LAP. Finally and most noteworthy, in recognition of her multilingual work Angelique was awarded The Prime Minister's Award for Excellence in Early Childhood Education in 2013.

LAP Journey 5: An English as a Second Language Teacher

Debbie Samson

'I am a multilingual teacher.'

Debbie is an experienced and professionally curious ESL teacher. Influenced by the work of Mary Ashworth (1998), she is aware of the richness of the language and literacy skills of newcomers. She is deeply concerned about language loss, the price they too often pay as they learn the classroom language. Guided by Ashworth's writing, Debbie strongly believes that the responsibility of the school is to extend the knowledge of newcomers, to help them grow and learn bilingually and to make them 'more' than they were when they arrived in their new Canadian school. She describes this additive approach to working with newcomers as the 'lens' that guides and directs her work.

Debbie's LAP journey started when she arrived at Beaver Valley School (hereafter BV), a highly diverse senior school (Grades 7 and 8), located in a high immigrant-refugee, low-income area in southern Ontario. At the time of writing, BV had a population of 503 students from six neighbouring 'feeder schools'. Newcomers from 33 different countries made up approximately 40% of the school population. These students spoke 36 different home languages. The five most widely spoken were Arabic, Serbian, Urdu, Romanian and Spanish. With very few exceptions, the BV teaching staff were monolingual speakers of English. Support for newcomers at BV consisted of one full-time ESL teacher (Debbie), limited part-time help (an ESL teacher and educational assistant) and a settlement worker who visited the school one day a week.

Soon after arriving at BV, Debbie observed a number of things about the newcomers that caused her to pause and reflect. She noted that they self-identified as learners of English, were reluctant to use their home languages in school and seemed ashamed of their backgrounds. She also noted that the teaching staff at the school adopted 'assimilative' instructional practice and identified newcomer students by their lack of English. In most cases, newcomers' prior knowledge and language abilities were disregarded as teachers focused on the teaching of English language and literacy skills. Newcomers were often described as 'struggling' and 'disengaged' and were considered linguistically unprepared to attend science and technology classes.

For Debbie, these observations were a professional 'trigger' which made her reflect on her own work with newcomers. She reviewed different instructional practices (assimilative, supportive and inclusive) adopted with newcomers. She realized that it was assimilative practice that was making BV newcomers 'less' than they were, failing to 'enhance their well-being and academic success' (Ashworth, 1998). She also realized that supportive practice, an approach she had adopted for many years, failed to meet the needs of newcomers because it focused on English and marginally acknowledged their prior knowledge and skills. Guided by Ashworth's idea that teachers have the power to challenge and improve, Debbie set out to make a change. She shared her concerns and ideas with colleagues and engaged them in discussions about newcomers. What followed was the gradual school-wide adoption of LAP. You can read about this in the LAP profiles section of this chapter.

LAP in Schools: Canada

(1) Beaver Valley team
(2) Halifax schools
(3) Thornwood team

The three profiles presented here all share the same learning context. They all come from Canadian schools and describe how teachers working in kindergarten, primary, junior and intermediate classrooms integrated LAP into their school agendas and also into the prescribed curriculum.

LAP School Profile 1: Beaver Valley Team

Debbie Samson

> 'Central to our journey were the voices of newcomers and their families and the belief in the importance of working collaboratively in our efforts to transform our school.'

In the LAP journeys, you read how Debbie, an English as a second language teacher from Beaver Valley (BV), a Canadian senior school (Grades 7 and 8), shared her teaching concerns with her colleagues. As a language activist, she advocated for change and improvement in teaching newcomers. This profile is the story of how Debbie's personal journey helped transform BV into an inclusive and multilingual school.

Teamwork

The newly created BV multilingual team consisted of the school principal, core subject teachers (language, history, geography, science and maths), the school administrators and the settlement worker. This newly formed group decided to 'change and do more' for newcomers. In their discussions they focused on newcomers' backgrounds, skills and strengths and the reasons they were disengaged from the curriculum.

A working agenda

The BV team started their multilingual work with four actions:

- building relationships;
- opening classroom doors to home languages and literacies;
- listening to newcomers; and
- bringing newcomers into the curriculum.

Action 1: Building relationships

Building relationships with colleagues, newcomers, families and the community was a priority for the BV team.

Learning and sharing with colleagues

In their discussions, the BV team acknowledged the fact that, historically, the Ontario education system was not designed to support newcomers' bilingualism. They agreed that the time has come to change this: to move away from monolingual teaching and work together to adopt LAP. Their work agenda included the following:

- identify newcomers' skills and strengths;
- engage in professional book study;
- share resources;
- apply for funding to support multilingual initiatives;
- collaborate with teachers in neighbouring schools and with school board members; and
- present at multilingual conferences.

Connecting with newcomer students

The BV team planned a number of topic-specific clubs (Welcoming Club, Lunch Club and Homeroom Class Buddies) to encourage newcomers to interact with their classmates. What started as a meeting and sharing time turned into a 'welcome and support' initiative, where students reached out to newcomers and helped them navigate their new school.

Another 'connecting' initiative was an identity project which was guided by the question, 'How did I get to be a member of this class?' In this activity, all the students, not just the newcomers, engaged in discussions about their family histories. For example, Indigenous students talked about Canada as their land, while others discussed their origins and their journeys to Canada. Students shared their languages and cultures and talked about the advantages of speaking more than one language. Response to the identity initiative was enthusiastic and positive. One BV teacher described the class discussions as a 'buzz of excitement and rich learning', where interest was high as students shared and connected. The students documented their ideas in English and in their home languages in 'Think Books', which were shared with classmates, teachers and families.

Reaching out to communities

Community outreach was an important part of the BV multilingual agenda. The team stepped outside the school to connect with families and local action groups. They worked with cultural groups, home literacy instruction volunteers, newcomer mothers, a mosque-based support group for Syrian refugees and a Saturday school programme for African-Canadian students and families. These outreach activities helped the BV teachers to:

- better understand the lives of newcomers;
- spread their inclusive, multilingual and multicultural message;
- extend and enrich their classroom multilingual teaching initiatives; and
- link students' school, home and community experiences.

Action 2: Opening classroom doors to home languages and literacies

To make the move from English-only (assimilative and supportive) to English-plus (inclusive, multilingual) practice, BV teachers opened their classroom doors to all languages. As they did so, they were surprised to discover that many newcomer students were hesitant and unwilling to use their home languages. In discussions, the teachers arrived at two possible reasons for this:

* Many newcomer students and families had experienced discrimination when they spoke their native languages outside their homes.
* Many parents held the 'either-or' view of languages, telling their children that continued use of the home language would delay the learning of English.

To help newcomers understand that their home languages are important and acceptable, the BV team engaged them in discussions about language and language learning and shared information about bilingualism with families.

Discussions about language

Class discussions focused on sharing, comparing and discovering one another's language. Topics of discussion included: language learning, bilingualism, language similarities and differences, writing scripts and text directionality. Interest in each other's languages was high and students took the initiative to make their home language seen and heard in the classrooms in four ways:

* adding home languages to the classroom writing display;
* labelling classroom materials;
* displaying charts with home languages; and
* teaching their home languages to each other.

Connecting with families

Information about bilingualism was shared with families. Letters in home languages were sent home explaining the importance of home languages, how a speaker's two languages work together, how strong skills in the home language help in the learning of English, and the new multilingual direction of the school. Families were encouraged to participate in school assignments and projects by providing translations of weekly word lists. Response was positive from both students and families, and home–school collaborations were strengthened.

> 'We appreciate as a family having been given the opportunity to be a part of such a diverse community. Evan has learned a lot from his fellow students simply from their stories and learning about different backgrounds. ... This is what a healthy community is about – inclusion not segregation based on racial or socio-economic background. This clearly is a trait that has been fostered by the staff at the school.'
>
> Parent

Action 3: Listening to newcomers

The multilingual action described here happened spontaneously. It brought to light the difficulties newcomer students often face. Deeply touched, Debbie turned this troubling situation into a powerful, transformative experience. Here's what happened.

'We are multi-language learners!'

In a chance conversation about English language support, Debbie discovered something that both surprised and shocked her. Abdullah, a Grade 8 newcomer, admitted that even though the BV English language support programme was helpful, the terms ESL (English as a second language) and ELL (English language learner) were hurtful and painful to him. He confessed that they made him feel like a 'stupid loser'. He told Debbie that these terms serve as a constant reminder of his limited English language ability. He also revealed that he had been bullied because he didn't speak 'good English'. For Abdullah, the acronyms ESL and ELL communicated a clear message: 'English is important. English is the language of the school. Other languages don't matter.' He also felt that ESL is inaccurate because for many newcomers, English is a third or a fourth language, and not a 'second' one.

Abdullah's comments about his experience and his dislike of the English-focused labels both surprised and troubled Debbie. It was only when he asked 'Why do we use ESL and ELL?' that she stopped and considered the question. She admitted that she too was uncomfortable with the terms. They both agreed that a new term was needed, one would that accurately and fairly portray newcomers.

When Abdullah coined the term **Many Language Learner** or **MLL**, Debbie thought it best to take this idea to the class for feedback. Sure enough, Abdullah's classmates confirmed his feelings about the limitations and unfairness of the terms ESL and ELL. They enthusiastically supported the use of MLL (Figure 3.5), but felt that 'many' should

Figure 3.5 Multi-language learners

be changed to 'multi' to make it sound 'more important'. Excitement was high as the newcomers proudly announced, 'I am a multi-language learner'. They shared their languages, took ownership of the new term and talked about changing English as a second language (ESL) to multi-language learning (MLL). The new term entered the school vocabulary and the use of ESL and ELL was discouraged.

Across BV classrooms, plans were put in place to promote and share the new term with the entire school community: students, teachers, families and the principal. Projects to share the transition from ESL to MLL included posters, poetry, artwork, testimonials, stories, a video and even an anthem. Two examples follow: poems and language-learning trees.

ESL and MLL poems

ESL = English-less stupid loser	Multi-language learner
That's how I feel ESL stands for. Being in ESL made me feel like a blind man in a crowd. Unable to do what everybody else could do. I tried to leave ESL as fast as possible. I wanted the same respect as everyone else. Outside of ESL I felt I no longer had to carry this 3-letter word around everywhere, letting people know that I don't know English. Leaving ESL I had to give up my background and my mother tongue. I turned my back on ESL and tried to forget about this – until I thought about MLL.	That's who we represent. We are the embodiment of two, three, four and even five languages. In MLL we can be who we are, we can take pride in who we are. In MLL I feel like I'm standing on top of a mountain looking at everyone who can only speak one language. I am proud to be a MLL because I know that not everybody in this world can speak two languages. I am a MLL! I am proud to be a MLL! I am proud to be a Multi-Language Learner!

Language learning trees

In a collaborative art project, a group of BV teachers, newcomers, parents and a Grade 8 student-artist decided that a tree would be the symbol to best represent their language learning experiences. As ideas and suggestions were put forward, two trees emerged, showing a learner of English and a learner of many languages.

The tree in Figure 3.6 represents the newcomer who is viewed as an English language learner. Like the tree, this student is forlorn and sad. Like the floating, rootless tree, the English language learner is cut off from country, family, culture, friends and language. Like the broken branches, the newcomer feels disengaged and detached. The hollow is empty and the birds are flying away from the tree. The colours are dark, foreboding and desolate. The tone is one of absence and loss.

In contrast, the multi-language learner (Figure 3.7) is cheerful and colourful. The tree is deep-rooted, strong and full of life. The healthy branches are full of birds and the hollow is inhabited. The dominant colour is green, a combination of the optimism and happiness of yellow and the calm of blue. The orange in the background radiates energy and warmth. This is the grounded, multi-language learner who is learning, growing and bursting with life.

Figure 3.6 English language learner

Figure 3.7 Multi-language learner

Of all the BV multilingual initiatives, the student-driven MLL name change and the language tree project were the most powerful and memorable. They helped transform BV into an inclusive multilingual environment, giving newcomers a voice.

Action 4: Bringing newcomers into the curriculum

The classroom discussions and activities described in the previous three 'actions' showed the BV teachers two things about newcomers:

- their knowledge is encoded in their home language; and
- English-only teaching prevents them from engaging in the curriculum and moving forward in their learning.

To make the curriculum accessible and relevant to newcomers, the BV team put the following strategies in place:

- extend curriculum topics to include the countries of origin of newcomer students;
- provide a language choice in class assignments and projects;
- encourage students who are speakers of the same home languages to work together; and
- provide multilingual technological support (keyboards, translators and story apps).

By adding a multilingual component to their lessons, the science and maths teachers in the two examples that follow ensured the engagement and participation of newcomers.

A multilingual science lesson

When the Grade 8 science teacher discovered that the newcomers had a great deal of knowledge about the water cycle, she made the lesson relevant to them by including information about water-related issues in their countries of origin. Instead of the usual English language summative assignment, she encouraged the students to work together, research water-related issues in their countries, construct a water purification system and prepare a multimodal, multi-language presentation of their work.

Multilingual maths

When Grade 7 newcomers reported that English maths vocabulary was unfamiliar and was making learning difficult, the teacher suggested a multilingual solution. She prepared charts of key maths vocabulary and concepts that students, parents and volunteers translated into their home languages. Completed multi-language maths charts were included in students' maths binders and used for reference.

Word alphabet books

Word alphabet books are an effective way of helping students articulate, document and share their experiences. They are particularly powerful with newcomers because they allow them to share their experiences about leaving home, arriving in a new country and learning a new language.

In the example that follows, Grade 7 and 8 newcomers from Somalia, Kenya, Syria, Lebanon, Turkey, Eritrea, Nepal, Egypt and Cuba were invited by Debbie to share their immigration experiences and prepare personal bilingual narratives and multimodal identity texts. They were encouraged to work together, consult resources and follow these instructions:

---

(1)   Choose a word that is important to you.
(2)   Match each letter of your selected word with a descriptor and an explanation.
(3)   Brainstorm with your classmates to plan your ideas.
(4)   Prepare a rough copy in two languages. Use translator apps or ask a classmate, parent or family member to help you with translations.
(5)   Edit your work and make the necessary changes.
(6)   Ask a classmate to edit your work.
(7)   Ask a teacher, parent or volunteer to edit your work.
(8)   Type your pages into Google Slides. Use one slide for each page.
(9)   Add visuals:
   • draw your pictures on paper, photograph them and put them into Google Slides;
   • use a tablet, phone, or camera to take pictures;
   • find pictures on the internet; and
   • obtain permission to include a photo of a friend, family member or teacher.
(10) Complete the 'About the author' page.
(11) Do a final edit of your book. Ask a classmate and the teacher to review your final copy.

Your book is now ready to be published and shared.

Debbie describes the purpose of the multilingual project as follows:

• gives newcomers a voice;
• allows them to share immigration experiences;
• brings them into the curriculum;
• allows them to work bilingually;
• encourages literacy;
• develops literacy skills in both school and home languages; and
• provides a sense of accomplishment and pride.

This project was an engaging and exciting experience for the newcomers. They selected words that were important to them, for example, money, Syria, football, peace, learning, family and education. They shared ideas and worked together. Bashaer, a Grade 7 newcomer from Syria, chose the word 'peace' and her home language (Arabic) and English to prepare her book. Two (English) pages from her Arabic-English book are presented here:

About the author

Hello, my name is Bashaer. I am in Grade 7. I am originally from the city of Damascus in Syria. I left Syria because of the war, and I went to Egypt. I lived in Egypt for four years. After four years I came to Canada. I am very happy I came to Canada because there was no peace in Egypt or Syria.

I now live in Canada. I can speak two languages, Arabic and English, and I am also learning French and Spanish from my friends.

If I had two wishes for the world they would be that there would be peace in all the world, and that all people would be happy. In my free time I like to read books and help my mother.

My book is about peace because I want peace in the world. When you read my book I hope you feel happy and peaceful. I also hope you think how important peace is to life and that peace is a blessing given to us by God. I hope my book wins your admiration.

Thank you so much for reading my book.

Peace

P is for peace

All my classmates think peace is important for the world. Rachel says: 'The world needs peace because people need peace to live.' Bourouj says: 'People need peace to be able to do what they enjoy and like.' Abdirahman says: 'Peace is important so countries will be safe and people will be friends.' I say: 'The world needs peace because the world is not safe without peace.'

E is for everywhere

We all need peace everywhere. Peace has an important role for everyone. Everyone wants peace. I personally want everyone to be safe. I don't want other countries to end up like my country Syria. Syria has been suffering for many years. For many years Syria has been unsafe. I want to give safety and peace to the whole world. I want all the kids in the world to be safe too.

A is for all

All people in the world want to have peace, but there are many countries, like my country, that don't have peace. People around the world want peace and safety. Families want their kids to be safe. For example, I have many cousins in Syria and I am very sad for them. I want peace for all the world.

C is for community

In order to bring peace to the world, we must start from the community. People in society must cooperate and help each other to have peace. We always need to work together and solve problems together. We must solve problems as one, and not blame each other, to spread peace in the world. We always need to protect each other so the world can be a safe place for everyone.

E is for enjoy
   We should enjoy our life, but we can't do that without peace. I want every kid in the world to be happy. We should have hope and we should be optimistic. The war will end and everybody will enjoy their life.

LAP School Profile 2: Multilingual Teaching in Halifax Schools

Sonja Grcic-Stuart

Immigration in Nova Scotia

Halifax is the capital city of Nova Scotia, an eastern (or Atlantic) Canadian province with a unique immigration history. For over 40 years, between 1928 and 1971, it served as the entry point or immigration gateway, referred to as Pier 21, admitting over one million newcomers who arrived mostly from Europe and settled across Canada.[1] Over the years, the number of newcomers who remained in Nova Scotia has dramatically changed. For example, between 1981 and 2005 retention rates dropped significantly as many newcomers arriving in Halifax moved on to other parts of Canada.[2] However, recent recruitment and integration initiatives at federal, provincial and community levels have encouraged newcomers to stay in Nova Scotia, raising retention rates to approximately 70%.

Today immigrants make up 5% of Nova Scotia's population. This figure is well below the Canadian average of 19%, making it an 'immigrant-scarce' province compared to more 'immigrant-rich' provinces such as Alberta, British Columbia, Ontario and Quebec.

'Diversity is reflected in our school populations'

Not surprisingly, the settling of immigrants in Nova Scotia is reflected in the schools. In the 2015–2016 school year, 5% of the student population or 2700 students attending Halifax schools (serving kindergarten to Grade 12) had immigrant status. These students arrived from 78 countries and spoke 60 different languages. The five most widely reported languages were Arabic, Tagalog, Chinese, Russian and Nepali. Approximately two-thirds of these newcomers were identified as English as an additional language (EAL) learners, requiring some level of English language support.

Sonja, the EAL consultant, who works directly with all 136 Halifax schools, describes the current teaching situation as 'very different' and 'exciting'. The arrival of newcomers challenges teachers, she reports, requiring them to 'change and adapt' their instructional practice to meet the needs of newcomers.

Instructional practice with newcomers in Halifax schools[3]

While approaches to working with newcomers vary across Halifax teachers and schools, supportive practice, or the teaching and learning of English together with the acknowledgement of home languages and celebrations of cultures, is adopted most widely.

Cultural celebrations are popular in Halifax schools. To help teachers in their cultural initiatives, 'culturally relevant pedagogy specialists' provide teachers with information about different cultures. The 12 schools included in this profile regularly organized cultural celebrations. In addition to annual welcome events for newcomer families, they celebrated Multicultural Nights and Multicultural Days which included 'ethnic dishes', costume, dance and music from different countries. Newcomer families and communities participated in these events and created flags and cultural displays.

An example of cultural celebrations is the Gaelic programme offered in response to the current revival of and interest in the Gaelic language. Today more than 1200 Nova Scotians speak Gaelic fluently. While students attend basic Gaelic language lessons, the main purpose of the programme is the exploration and study of Gaelic culture.

Classroom teachers reported that celebrating cultures helped them better understand newcomers and connect with newcomer families and communities. It also helped them move beyond assimilative or English-only practice and journey towards supportive practice. They described supportive practice as a 'more open and accepting way of teaching newcomers' that creates a 'real sense of school community' and remains 'a part of just about everything that we do'. For some Halifax teachers, the cultural celebrations sparked an interest in newcomers' language and literacy skills. This led them to review their current practice and think about multilingual teaching.

Province-wide multilingual efforts and initiatives (workshops, conferences and sharing of resources) organized by the EAL team introduced Halifax teachers to LAP. Overall, response was positive, as seen in the increasing number of teachers and principals who are looking beyond supportive practice and adopting multilingual teaching.

The four LAP actions described here come from Halifax classrooms with newcomer populations ranging from 6% to 25%. The final LAP action is a school board initiative.

Action 1: Making home languages visible

Halifax teachers who were new to multilingual teaching closely followed the suggestions found in LAP12. One of the first things they did was to make home languages visible in the classroom. They documented children's home languages and, together with the children, prepared charts, such as the multilingual Hello sign (Figure 3.8). These were then displayed in the classroom.

Figure 3.8 A multilingual hello sign

Action 2: Making home languages seen and heard

As interest in multilingual teaching grew, home languages were both seen and heard in Halifax classrooms. Here are three examples:

- daily school news was delivered in English and in home languages;
- dual-language books were added to classroom and school libraries; and
- parents visited classrooms to share dual-language books.

Action 3: Home languages included in the curriculum

In some Halifax classrooms, teachers brought home languages directly into the curriculum. They invited newcomers to participate in rich tasks using their home languages. Supported by technological resources (computers, electronic translators, multilingual keyboards and computer applications), the curriculum became both accessible and meaningful to newcomers. Here are two examples.

In the first example (Figure 3.9), a Korean-speaking newcomer, with the help of the teacher, created a Korean-English counting chart. In the second example (Figure 3.10), a newcomer created a bilingual science chart listing the seasons of the year in Japanese and in English.

Teachers reported that these experiences engaged newcomers and gave them a sense of purpose and belonging. Above all, using the home language in lessons, projects and assignments communicated a very powerful message to newcomers: 'I can participate using what I know.'

Action 4: Welcome to our school – Welcome to Canada

These two YouTube clips were created to welcome and integrate newcomers:

- In this short YouTube clip, Sonja, the EAL consultant of the Halifax school board, talks about welcoming, supporting and integrating newcomers. She describes

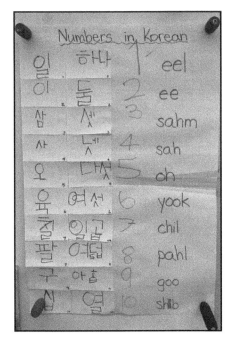

Figure 3.9 Korean-English counting chart

Figure 3.10 English-Japanese science project

how the new arrivals have both changed and enriched the schools of Halifax: https://www.youtube.com/watch?v=kvlALY1mHUQ.
- This YouTube clip was created by Grade 6 Halifax students to welcome Syrian arrivals: https://www.youtube.com/watch?v = kvlALY1mHUQ.

LAP School Profile 3: Thornwood Team

Gillian Caron, Roberto Di Prospero, Lynn Desharnais, Meagan Geddes, Kristen McGinn, Safiya Shere, Susan Stuckless and Tobin Zikmanis[4]

This profile describes the work of the Thornwood School (hereafter TW) multilingual teaching team and is presented in four parts:

- Part 1: Background
- Part 2: Sustaining, enriching and extending multilingual teaching
- Part 3: Welcoming and integrating newly arrived children from Syria
- Part 4: Launching a summer multilingual programme

Part 1: Background

TW is a linguistically diverse kindergarten to Grade 5 public school located in Mississauga, a large regional municipality of southern Ontario (Canada). The TW multilingual team consists of classroom teachers, the school librarian, the special education teacher, the English as a second language teacher, the school settlement worker and the principal. With its longstanding tradition of multilingual teaching, TW teachers strongly believe that children arrive in school with the 'totality of their life experiences' (Cummins, 2018) and a skillset that includes cultural and social knowledge, language ability and an understanding of literacy and numeracy. In TW classrooms, these skills are acknowledged, extended and viewed as important learning and teaching resources.

Over the years, TW teachers have participated in many research and instructional practice partnerships and collaborations. Their school has an international reputation for excellence in multilingual pedagogy and is considered the go-to example of inclusive and innovative work with newcomer children and families.

In the late 1990s, a group of TW teachers collaborated with education researchers, pre-service teachers, graduate students, families and community members in an action research project. The purpose of the project was to identify the language and literacy learning needs of newcomers and develop effective instructional strategies. Initiatives were put in place to integrate and engage newcomers. One of these initiatives was the Multilingual Story Project, which led to the development of the Dual Language Showcase website. This active website showcases dual-language storybooks created by children in 28 languages.[5]

The action research project came to an end, but the TW teachers continue their commitment to supporting newcomer children and families. They remain open, responsive and dedicated to 'ongoing improvement and enhancement of protocols and activities associated with the reception and orientation of new students' (Schecter & Cummins, 2003).

'Teaching through a multilingual lens' (Cummins & Persad, 2014) remains a guide for TW teachers. Always on the lookout for new information, they attend workshops, lectures and conferences, updating and expanding their knowledge about multilingual teaching and learning. The leadership of Roberto, the TW principal, is both noteworthy and exemplary. Rarely found in his office, he walks through the school hallways, greeting children (whose names he knows) in their home languages or with a cheery 'ciao' (his native Italian), offering high-fives. He visits classrooms, chats with the children, listens to their stories and applauds their accomplishments and successes. His office time is often interrupted by groups of children who come to share their projects.

The TW language landscape

At the end of the 2016–2017 school year, TW children spoke a total of 36 home languages. The five most widely used were Arabic, English, Urdu, Hindi and Tamil. The arrival of the Syrian families increased the number of Arabic-speaking children from 13% in 2014 to 29% in 2017. English was reported as the home language for 25% of the children, Urdu was spoken by 17%, while the percentages for Hindi and Tamil were 5% and 4%, respectively. The Other (20%) category included the following 30 languages: Albanian, Bengali, Bosnian, Chinese (Mandarin, Cantonese), Croatian, Dari, Farsi, French, Gujarati, Kannada, Kiswahili, Korean, Malayalam, Marathi, Pashto, Polish, Portuguese, Punjabi, Romanian, Russian, Serbian, Somali, Spanish, Tagalog, Tamil, Telugu, Tigrinya, Turkish, Ukrainian and Vietnamese.

Part 2: Sustaining, enriching and extending multilingual teaching

 Of the many LAP actions and initiatives launched by the TW multilingual teaching team, five are described here.

Action 1: Newcomers are far more than learners of the school language

When they talk about newcomer children, the TW team tries to avoid using traditional English-focused labels such as ESL and ELL. They are sensitive to the fact that newcomers are 'far more than learners of the classroom language' (Chumak-Horbatsch, 2012) and that they arrive with language and literacy skills. The TW team admits that it is not easy to change the ESL and ELL labels because they are so widely used. However, they believe that it is important to 'change the channel' and use terms that accurately and fairly describe the dual- or multi-language status of newcomers.

Action 2: Language of the month

Language of the month is an ongoing collaborative project. TW children, families and teachers work together to showcase the home languages of the school community. Displays include photos, maps, stories, writing samples, lists of speakers and common

Figure 3.11 Language of the month: Italian

words (Figure 3.11). The completed display is given a special place in the school hallway and is shared with the school community and also with visitors.

TW teachers report that the Language of the month display is a popular place. Children often stop by to talk about the contents and ask each other about their home languages. One teacher reported that two children, speakers of Indonesian and Buryat (a variety of Mongolian), asked that their languages be featured, even though they were the only speakers of these languages.

Action 3: Classroom language policy

To guide classroom language use and behaviours, TW teachers worked with children to create language policies or lists of 'rules and expectations' (Figure 3.12). Teachers reported that this activity started with a general discussion about rules and regulations and led to comments about specific classroom guidelines. Children agreed

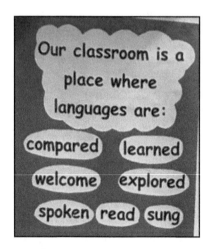

Figure 3.12 Classroom language policy

Figure 3.13 The word 'peace' in home languages

that language rules are important to help everyone, especially the newcomers, 'feel safe and happy'.

Action 4: School assemblies

School assemblies are important events at TW. During these monthly gatherings, the school community comes together to connect, share information, recognize achievements and celebrate special days and events. Over the past years, home languages have been included in TW assembly programmes. For example, newcomers are invited to participate and make announcements in their home languages. Figure 3.13 shows children at a Remembrance Day celebration holding signs with the word 'peace' written in their home languages.[6]

Action 5: What's in a name?

In a number of TW classrooms, bilingual name cards were used as a starting point for a name discovery activity (Figure 3.14). This started with discussions about different terms associated with names such as surname, last name, family name, given name, nickname, pet name and hypocorism.[7] Topics of discussion included the meanings of names, pronunciations, translations and different ways of saying the same name. For example, the name John is Jean in French, Juan in Spanish, Giovanni in Italian and Ivan in Ukrainian. When teachers saw that children had little information about their own names, they turned to families for help (see sample letter). This activity proved to be interesting for both children and families. Children were fascinated by the fact that names have origins and meanings, and families happily shared information about names.

Figure 3.14 Bilingual name cards

Sample letter to parents

Dear Parents,

We are currently learning about names.

Please take the time to talk to your child about his or her name, its meaning and why it was selected. Together with your child, please answer the five questions below.

1. Our home language or languages: _____

2. Child's name in English: _____

3. Child's name in home language: _____

4. Meaning of my child's name: _____

5. Reason(s) the name was selected: _____

_____

Thank you.

Part 3: Welcoming and integrating children from Syria

'This was a unique educational experience and I wanted to be a part of it.'

TW teacher

Background

The year 2015–2016 was extraordinary for the TW school community. The arrival of children from war-torn Syria was an unforeseen and unexpected challenge for the teachers. The following questions dominated staff meetings and classroom discussions as the TW community prepared and planned for the arrival of the newcomers:

- Who are these children?
- Do they speak English?
- How do we welcome them?
- How do we create a safe space for them?
- Do they all speak Arabic?
- How many are arriving?
- How many will be in my class?

The multilingual teaching team met regularly to talk about strategies to welcome and integrate the new arrivals. They consulted a number of resources (CMAS, 2015) to understand the travel and transition circumstances of the newcomers. Strategies were put in place and ideas were shared. Each classroom buzzed with discussions about the background of the newcomers, their reasons for leaving Syria, their language and culture, prior schooling, the challenges of leaving home and ways to help, include and support them. Excitement, energy and anticipation ran high as TW awaited the arrival of the Syrian children.

The Syrian families started to arrive in the fall of 2015, and by the spring of 2016, 76 children from 41 government-sponsored families were enrolled in their new school. During the TW orientation and tour, teachers, interpreters and student Language Ambassadors (Arabic-speaking children) were on hand to greet and welcome the newcomers. Families were given an orientation package (in Arabic) which included information about the school, the Ontario education and health systems, Canada's food guide, literacy and numeracy guides, tips for winter dressing and the settlement worker's contact information.

Background information available to the teachers revealed that the displacement and travel story was different for each Syrian family. For example, some left war-torn Syria and lived in refugee camps in neighbouring countries of asylum such as Lebanon, Jordan and Turkey. Some of the children had their schooling interrupted, while others had experienced war-related horrors and trauma.

Early behaviours

The early behaviours of the newcomers from Syria present a picture of eager, anxious but happy children who found themselves in a new place surrounded by affection, support and help. Here are some examples:

You don't speak Arabic?
The younger newcomers (kindergarten and primary level) were surprised and at times shocked to discover that people in their new school did not understand or speak Arabic.

Smiles and hugs always work!
The newly arrived children responded very positively to smiles, laughter, humour, jokes and hugs. The TW teachers speculated that these may have been in short supply during their journey to Canada.

'I love school ...'
Overall, the newcomers were very happy to be in school. Parents reported that their children were disappointed that their new school was closed at weekends.

'I want to learn English because all people speak English.'
Most of the newcomers were anxious and excited to learn English. In some cases, they refused to use Arabic.

My language has a place here.
The arrival of the newcomers served as a 'language trigger' for the entire school. It further validated the multilingual teaching agenda and confirmed the fact that all home languages are welcome in TW. Hearing Arabic prompted many children to step forward, identify and showcase their own home language skills.

More is better!
Single newcomers often felt uncertain and overwhelmed in their new classroom. With the arrival of other newcomers, they opened up and were more confident.

Go away!
First uses of English were mimicked commands such as: 'Come here!' 'Go away!' 'Hurry up!' 'Shut up!'

Let me help!
The TW children were quick to welcome and help. In the following example a non-Arabic speaking teacher was trying to explain the importance of warm clothing to a Syrian father who spoke little English. The teacher spoke slowly, pointed to the door and used hand gestures to get his message across. A TW child overheard this encounter, stopped and said: 'I can help, I speak Arabic.' In a matter of minutes, the father smiled, nodded and said 'Shukraan' (Thank you) to the teacher and the helpful interpreter.

Integrating newcomers

The English as a second language teachers guided the integration of the newcomers. They organized weekly meetings, called Knowledge Building Circles, where the TW team shared resources, raised concerns, identified challenges and discussed effective measures to integrate the newcomers and monitor their transition. The team helped individual teachers by providing in-class support. They also worked with small groups of newcomers who needed breaks from their new classrooms.

Early activities with newcomers included movement-based and fun games that encouraged participation and interaction. During these games, children were invited to speak Arabic and attempt words in English. For example, as the children sat in a circle rolling a soccer ball to each other, the teacher called them by name, provided the words of her accompanying actions (roll, move, pick up, your turn), encouraged them to repeat the words and asked for and attempted equivalents in Arabic.

Teachers also provided newcomers with age- and level-appropriate 'rich tasks' or relevant and meaningful activities that activated their prior knowledge and, as reported by Safiya, an English as a second language teacher, 'honoured what they already know and arrive with'. They paired the newcomers with Arabic-speaking classmates, provided Arabic-English resources, encouraged the use of visuals to accompany their written work and created Arabic-English word lists and texts.

Part 4: Summer camp

The school year did not end in June for one group of TW newcomers. They took part in a summer programme that focused on language, multiliteracy and numeracy. With its hands-on approach, the programme, called Summer Adventure in Literacy (SAIL), included field trips and cooking classes, art activities, outdoor sports and water play. According to Kristen (Figure 3.15), one of the SAIL teachers and an outspoken advocate of multilingual teaching, the summer camp provided continuity for the children, allowing them to extend and build on their language, numeracy and literacy skills.

Figure 3.15 Kristen, a SAIL teacher

Figure 3.16 I love Canada

With the help of an Arabic-speaking assistant, Kristen encouraged the SAIL camp children to create Arabic-English word lists and prepare bilingual stories and identity texts. The response of the children was positive. They said that having fun, making friends and learning English were important to them. One nine-year-old girl, who wrote I LOVE CANADA on the blackboard (Figure 3.16), reported that 'It is safe here, but it's not safe back in Syria'. Already literate in her new language, she vowed to improve by reading an English book every day.

LAP in Schools: Germany, Iceland, Luxembourg and Sweden

(4) A kindergarten classroom
(5) Icelandic preschools
(6) Luxembourg classrooms
(7) A school in Sweden

The four profiles presented here describe how teachers transformed their classrooms and schools into multilingual centres, and integrated newcomers and brought them into the curriculum.

LAP School Profile 4: A Linguistically Diverse Kindergarten Classroom

Helen Arnold

'I love inquiry-driven learning – you find out so many new things and the children are so interested. You never know where the inquiry will lead.'

This profile takes us to Helen's kindergarten classroom. Located in an international school in Germany, where the language of programme delivery is English, this school offers a comprehensive programme of academic studies and extracurricular activities for kindergarten to Grade 12. The home languages of the four- and five-year-old children in Helen's class included two English speakers and 11 children who spoke the following seven home languages: German, Arabic, Korean, Chinese, Hindi, Turkish and French (1).

In keeping with her inquiry-based teaching approach, Helen scaffolds the children's language exploration and learning. She guides their language experiences and helps them extend their understanding of language concepts. This approach is directly in line with the prescribed International Baccalaureate (IB) young learners curriculum which views young children as natural inquirers.

Four things stand out in Helen's teaching:

- She is a multilingual educator who is fluent in English, Russian, German, Slovak and Spanish; she also has a beginning proficiency in Arabic, Italian and Korean.
- She shares her knowledge and love of languages with the children. She encourages the children to engage in language inquiry and showcase and share their language knowledge and skills.
- Her professional curiosity is high and she is always looking for new teaching ideas. She regularly attends conferences to keep up with new developments in childhood bilingualism and multilingual teaching.
- She strongly believes in the bilingual potential of children who do not speak the classroom language. She avoids labels like 'additional-language learner' and refers to non-English speaking children as 'emergent bilinguals'.

 The five LAP actions that follow show how Helen follows children's interests. She takes on the role of learner and guides the children from wondering about the world around them to a 'position of enacted understanding and further questioning' (Scardamalia, 2002).

Action 1: A friendly police officer in India and a red fireboat in Venice!

Before a visit to the local police station, Helen wanted to find out how well the children understood the concept of police officer. Using a picture of two German police officers standing beside a police car, she asked an open-ended question: 'What do you see?' Ignoring the question, one child answered: 'I saw a friendly policeman in India.' This response triggered a lot of interest and many questions from the other children: 'How did he look?' Building on this interest, Helen suggested they work together to find a picture of a police officer from India. The results of a group internet search were projected on the classroom interactive whiteboard. When a child announced 'Now policeman in China!' they did another internet search and added a Chinese policeman to their poster (Figure 3.17).

Figure 3.17 Police officers in different countries

When 'firefighter' was the topic of discussion, the children wanted to know about fire engines in different countries. They once again searched the internet to find photos and facts about fire engines in the children's countries of birth and origin. They were excited to see different sizes and shapes of fire engines. While looking at fire truck images, the children noticed a red boat, which they quickly called 'a fire boat!' Sure enough, it was a fireboat used in Venice. This led to a discussion about Venice. Children were captivated by the idea of canals and boats.

Action 2: Language concepts and vocabulary

Helen explicitly teaches language concepts and vocabulary. She uses bilingual name cards to remind children that they are speakers of two languages. She engages them in discussion and provides the English names of their home languages. She uses maps and globes to locate the countries where their languages are spoken. She also talks about the many different ways people speak and write. The example that follows shows how Helen provides words (China, Chinese) to help the children articulate language facts.

Helen points to a bilingual name card.

Child: Back! Look back!

Helen turns the name card over.

Child: China! Chinese!

Helen: That's right, Lillian, you come from China. That's how we write your name in Chinese.

Interactions such as these encouraged the children to identify and read their own bilingual name cards and those of their friends. When Helen suggested sorting the bilingual name cards, the children sorted by country ('Korea and Korea, same, same!'). They also offered words that started with the same letters as the countries ('Korea – kite'). This both surprised and delighted Helen.

The bilingual name card activity started out as a brief morning 'circle' discussion and turned into something 'very engaging and dynamic'. Helen adjusted the daily schedule to give children time to order, sort, identify, share and collaborate.

Action 3: The teacher as language learner – what does chadz mean?

Helen is always ready to take on the role of language learner. One day she was listening to two children speaking Mandarin during lunchtime. She heard a word that sounded like tsadze. Thinking back to an earlier experience with this word, she asked the children whether tsadze means 'cook'. The children laughed, held up a fork and said, 'No, this is tsadze!' Unsure of the pronunciation, Helen searched the internet, asking 'How do you say fork in Mandarin?' She discovered that it is pronounced chadz. Thanking the children, she told them, 'You are my Chinese teachers!' A Korean child standing nearby added, 'I am Korea teacher!', to which Helen replied, 'Yes, you are my Korean teacher!'

Action 4: Mother-tongue mornings

On mother-tongue mornings, school staff, visitors and families come to Helen's classroom to share languages and cultures. She plans a weekly morning session together with the families, guides the discussions and has resources on hand to illustrate, highlight and follow up on the shared experiences.

In one mother-tongue session, the mother (a speaker of Turkish and German) of newcomer Alara, together with an English-speaking cousin, visited the classroom to talk about Turkish culture, language and food.

After locating Turkey and Germany on the map, the children viewed images of Alara's hometown on the computer screen and talked about mountains and the sea. While Helen communicated with Alara's mother in German, the English-speaking

Figure 3.18 Turkish food poster

cousin served as interpreter. The children talked about distance, direction and travel. They concluded that Turkey is very far away from Germany. Helen then asked the children about modes of transportation: 'How did Alara get to Germany?' The children suggested a car, a train and an aeroplane. Alara's mother confirmed that they had indeed travelled to Germany by plane. They discussed Turkish words, traditional Turkish dress and Turkish food (Figure 3.18). As the children prepared Turkish bread called pogača, they learned that lezzetli in Turkish means 'yummy' or 'delicious'.

Helen reported that the children were 'totally absorbed' during the 40-minute visit and that Alara was 'proud and happy, chatting in Turkish'.

Action 5: My country in a box

A letter was sent home, asking parents to fill an empty shoebox with items that characterized the family's country (or countries) of origin or the child's country of birth. Helen provided a list of suggestions such as flags, banners, maps, coins, books, newspapers, flyers, non-perishable foods, musical instruments, CDs, DVDs, toys, photos, pieces of clothing, postcards and posters. Parents and children presented the country boxes to the class. Some parents brought additional objects and information to share with the class. The discussions were lively and children had many questions about the contents of the boxes. Helen was on internet standby when child presenters needed help – for example, to provide the name, spelling and pronunciation of won or 원, the name of the South Korean currency. The results of the searches were displayed on the interactive whiteboard for all to see. Figure 3.19 shows a child explaining the contents of her German box: pretzel, books, coins, flag, chocolate, candy and dress (dirndl). Completed country boxes were labelled with the children's photos and made available for individual and group sharing.

Figure 3.19 German box

The children's interest in the country boxes was documented and integrated into ongoing Units of Inquiry. For example, the children created multilingual stories about objects in the country boxes. They also made multilingual word lists and added different currencies in their numeracy inquiry activities.

LAP School Profile 5: Multilingualism in Icelandic Preschools

Fríða Bjarney Jónsdóttir and Drífa Þórarinsdóttir

The changing language landscape of Iceland

Iceland is a Nordic country located between Europe and North America. It covers an area of 103,000 square kilometres and has a population of 330,000. The official language is Icelandic, a North Germanic language descended from Old Norse. Like Europe, Canada and the United States, Iceland has recently experienced demographic changes. In the last decade, the number of immigrants has increased significantly, transforming the country from homogeneous and monolingual to heterogeneous and multilingual. Approximately 100 different non-Icelandic languages are spoken in Iceland today, with Polish being the most widely used. While some newcomers settle in Icelandic coastline villages, most live in or near the capital city of Reykjavík.

Not surprisingly, these demographic changes are reflected in Icelandic preschools, where linguistic and cultural diversity is on the rise. Currently, 11% of all preschool children (aged one to six) have a non-Icelandic home language (Hagstofa Íslands, 2015). In Reykjavík, the number is even higher: approximately 19% or 1300 of the 7000 children attending preschools speak one or more non-Icelandic languages at home (Reykjavíkurborg, 2016). While the linguistic background of these children is quite diverse, the number from Polish-speaking homes is the highest.

Preschools in Iceland

Preschool or leikskóli is the first non-compulsory level in the educational system of Iceland (Icelandic Parliament, 2008). Most children (96%) in Iceland attend preschools. Preschools follow a national play-based curriculum (Icelandic Ministry of Education, Science and Culture, 2011) and are responsible for the care and education of young children, regardless of their ability, religion, language or background. The preschool curriculum emphasizes children's overall development, parental engagement and the development of Icelandic language and literacy. It focuses on social justice and urges teachers to meet the challenges of Iceland's changing population. However, supporting newcomer children and families is new to most Icelandic teachers, who are asking for guidance and resources.

Research on the education of newcomers

Research on the education of newcomers in Iceland is on the increase (Arnbjörnsdóttir, 2008, 2010; Jónsdóttir, 2011; Ólafsdóttir, 2010, 2015; Ragnarsdóttir, 2015; Þórðardóttir, 2012; Gunnþórsdóttir et al., in press). There is growing concern that newcomers are overrepresented in language intervention programmes. For example, in 2015 newcomers accounted for 51% of all children diagnosed with language impairment in Reykjavík preschools, and almost 80% of older newcomers (aged 7–16) in Reykjavík compulsory schools required educational support (Reykjavíkurborg, 2015). Also, the high dropout rates among newcomers in upper secondary schools show that these students, for whom Icelandic is a second or additional language, have not acquired the necessary knowledge and skills to succeed (Jónsson, 2013; Icelandic Government, 2009).

Educators and researchers are working together to better understand newcomer children and families. For example, in a recent study (Gunnþórsdóttir et al., in press), researchers at the University of Akureyri, in northern Iceland, interviewed teachers and newcomer parents to discover how each group viewed the education of newcomer children. They found that teachers had little support in their work with newcomers. They also found that there was a mismatch between Icelandic education delivery and teaching approaches and the more traditional, structured views of many newcomer parents. Finally, they noted a lack of collaboration and communication between newcomer homes and the school. The study ends with a call for 'supportive networks' and active collaboration.

Icelandic educational policy on young newcomers

Since 2001 the Reykjavík City Department of Education and Youth has focused on the integration and education of preschool-aged newcomers. The first multicultural policy for preschools was published in 2001 and updated in 2006. In 2013 a language and literacy policy was issued. It focused on emergent literacy in preschools, with special attention to bilingual children (Hjartardottir, 2013). That same year, the Committee on Icelandic as an Official Language presented recommendations to provide educators with tools to work with newcomer children and support their home language (Íslensk Málnefnd, 2013). The 2014 policy document entitled 'The World is Here!' (Reykavík City Department of Education and Youth, 2014) is considered a 'guiding light' for working with newcomers. The following passage from this document emphasizes the importance of newcomers' dual-language development:

> The goal is that all children succeed in Icelandic, as the ability to speak Icelandic is the main ground for democratic participation and equality in Icelandic society. All children whose first language is not Icelandic should have the opportunity to develop active bilingualism, i.e. gain the ability to maintain and strengthen their first language/s while at the same time achieving progress in learning the Icelandic language. (Reykavík City Department of Education and Youth, 2014: 6)

A recently published long-term action plan (2016–2019) highlights the importance of developing resources for teachers who work with newcomers. It emphasizes the need to support the teaching of Icelandic as a second language and the continued development of newcomers' home languages (Icelandic Parliament, 2015).

Working with newcomers in Icelandic preschools

Across Iceland, preschool teachers are adjusting their practice and opening their classroom doors to newcomer children and their families. Current multilingual initiatives include:

- documenting home languages;
- organizing bilingualism and multilingualism workshops and conferences;
- celebrating International Mother Language Day; and
- supporting newcomer families by adding translation features to school blogs and websites.

Creating and sharing dual-language books

In addition to the above multilingual initiatives, Icelandic preschool teachers report that creating and sharing dual-language books (Ada & Campoy, 2003; Bernhard *et al.*, 2006, 2008) is an effective and engaging way to connect with newcomer children and families. These book activities begin with group discussions about home artefacts (photos, objects, toys, drawings, posters, CDs, DVDs and books) provided by families. These are then used in the collaborative preparation of simple booklets or family identity texts (Cummins & Early, 2011). In these books, children's documented experiences are accompanied by captions, in both Icelandic and home languages. Many dual-language books turn into ongoing projects. They travel between home and preschool, where parents add entries about important events in the lives of their children.

Icelandic preschool teachers described dual-language books as an 'engaging power-ful tool' (Personal communication with Fríða Bjarney Jónsdóttir, 2017). They reported that this collaborative activity helped them better understand newcomer children, linked the home and the preschool, established partnership with newcomer families, and created spaces for home languages in the preschool.

The children were excited about their dual-language books, talked about them, 'read' them repeatedly, shared them with their friends and copied the captions. The response from parents was also positive, as noted in the following comment:

> '... we have a book and Dina was bringing pictures from preschool to home and we were putting photos from home in the book and everything was in this book and we wrote in our language and in Icelandic so that was a good idea to discuss every-thing what is going on in the school and in the home.'

LAP in Leikskólinn Krílakot

Leikskólinn (preschool) Krílakot is a colourful, bright and happy place located in Dalvík, a village in northern Iceland. The population of Dalvík and the surrounding Dalvíkurbyggð fishing and farming area is approximately 2000. In 1980 Leikskólinn Krílakot (hereafter LK) started as a small public school that served 50 children and fami-lies. There are currently 100 children and 30 teachers at LK. The children are divided into two groups: younger (aged nine months to three years) and older (aged four to six years).

The recent influx of immigrants has changed the language landscape of both Dalvík and LK. Icelandic is the home language of the majority (72%) of the children, and more than a quarter (28%) speak a language other than Icelandic in the home. This number is higher than in the capital city of Reykjavík,

More than half of the LK newcomer families (55%) speak Polish. The rest speak one or more of the following seven languages: Latvian, Thai, Filipino, Spanish, Russian, Arabic and English. Drifa, the principal of LK, reports that some Icelandic-born new-comers are exposed to more than one home language and Icelandic. For example, in one family the children are exposed to four languages: Icelandic in the preschool, Polish with their mother, Spanish with their Guatemalan father and English between the par-ents. Like the LK children, the staff are mostly speakers of Icelandic (87%), with various levels of proficiency in English. A small number of the teachers are also speakers of Polish, Filipino, Finnish and Danish. Of these, only two languages, Polish and Filipino, match the children's home languages.

Drifa describes multilingual teaching as a 'work in progress'. She emphasizes the importance of moving in 'small steps', to give teachers time to process two things: the changing language reality of Dalvík and LK, and the need to review and retool their instructional practice. While early LAP initiatives focused on introducing and explain-ing multilingual teaching to families and teachers, the three actions described here focus on professional collaborations, partnering with newcomer families and creating spaces for home languages and literacies.

Action 1: Professional and community outreach

Describing their northern location as 'isolated', Dalvíkurbyggð educators have made professional outreach a priority. They have responded to the change in demographics and the diversity of their classrooms by engaging in fact-finding missions and collecting multilingual resources and ideas. They collaborate with colleagues, researchers, policymakers and curriculum writers in Reykjavík and in countries with long-standing histories of immigration, such as Canada, the United States and Europe. For example, in 2013 a Dalvíkurbyggð educational consultant travelled to the Netherlands to attend a workshop that focused on adapting 'Story Sacks',[8] a collaborative literacy project, to a multilingual context. In 2014, a Dalvíkurbyggð delegation attended the author's LAP presentation at the International Association for Intercultural Education conference in Toronto.

Action 2: Partnering with newcomer families

When newcomer families register their children in preschool, they are given the following information about children's dual-language and literacy development:

- Home languages are important for children's overall development.
- Sharing books and stories regularly with children in the home language is important.
- Familiarity with literacy helps children succeed in school.
- Children who are confident and fluent in their home language will learn Icelandic without difficulty.
- Maintaining the home language and adding Icelandic will make children bilingual.

The principal of LK reported that newcomer families participate in multilingual projects and initiatives. For example, they attend meetings, provide translations, create multilingual resources, share information about their languages and writing systems and contribute artefacts for class discussions.

Action 3: Making home languages seen and heard in LK

Home languages are visible in the LK hallways and in the classrooms. Flags from children's countries of origin are displayed and materials and furniture have multilingual labels (Figure 3.20). Multilingual posters and drawings prepared by children, teachers and families decorate the hallway walls. Teachers also encourage children to use their home languages in the classroom.

Children's response

Children's response to the presence of home languages and literacies in LK has been positive and enthusiastic. For example, initially uncertain and hesitant newcomers came

Figure 3.20 Multilingual sign on the principal's door

to understand that there is a place for their languages in their new school. Icelandic-speaking children were fascinated by the fact that some of their classmates do not know Icelandic and are speakers of other languages. They asked for and often repeated words and numbers in the languages of their friends. In one case a four-year-old Icelandic-speaking boy told his teacher that he too speaks 'another language'. When asked to identify and speak the language, he produced gibberish sounds. The teacher explained this as the child's response to the class discussion about the value and advantages of speaking more than one language.

LAP School Profile 6: Multilingualism in Luxembourg Classrooms

Claudine Kirsch

This profile reports on the work of Claudine, an education researcher from the University of Luxembourg, whose topic of investigation is language practices and language behaviours in Luxembourg schools. With the encouragement and support of the Ministry of Education, she set out to develop and promote inclusive and innovative methods of language teaching. First, here is some background.

Luxembourg: One country – three official languages – and more …

Luxembourg is a small country (population 590,000) in the centre of Europe. Bordered by Belgium, Germany and France, Luxembourg has a unique language landscape with three official and administrative languages: Luxembourgish, German and French. The national language is Luxembourgish, the laws are in French, and the languages of the government are Luxembourgish, German and French. The three languages are spoken to varying extents and function as languages for working, writing and communicating, both formally and informally.

Non-official languages are also part of the language landscape of Luxembourg. For example, English is the fourth most common language, and Italian has been heard in Luxembourg since 1875 and Portuguese since the mid-1960s.[9] More recently, immigrants have added their languages (Japanese, Arabic, Russian, Pashto and Dari) to the Luxembourg language map.

Languages in Luxembourg schools

All three official languages are used in Luxembourg schools. Their use is separate, compartmentalized and grade-level specific (Kirsch, 2018; Kirsch & Bes, 2019). Even though 'multilingual' education recently became compulsory in early education, Luxembourgish is still the main language used in preschool (Leclerc, 2008). It is intended to lay the foundation for German, which is one of the languages of programme delivery in the primary grades. In the second primary year, the oral teaching of French begins, and the written form is introduced in the following year. From the age of seven, education is in Luxembourgish and German, and nearly half of the teaching time is given to language learning. French then progressively replaces German and becomes the main language of instruction in grammar school or secondary education (Weber & Horner, 2008). Proficiency in several languages is required for graduation from secondary school.

Opening the classroom doors to home languages

Guided by the social constructivist and dynamic bilingualism theories (García & Li Wei, 2014), Claudine opened the doors of preschool and primary classrooms to home languages. She provided the children with a flexible and open-ended story app called iTEO[10] (Kirsch & Bes, 2019), and created a 'safe and meaningful learning environment' which allowed them to do two things: create and share stories and move freely between languages. She documented the response behaviours of children and teachers. This is what she discovered.

Children's behaviours
- used the story app in creative ways;
- moved across Luxembourgish, home languages and the languages of classmates;
- used home languages when faced with gaps in Luxembourgish;
- used home languages to support classmates;
- worked collaboratively: created stories, made language decisions and supported each other;
- became aware of their language abilities and skills; and
- worked on their dual-language identity.

Teachers' behaviours
- taught greetings in children's home languages;
- sang in home languages (Portuguese, Italian, Albanian, English, Russian, Vietnamese, Chinese and Kirundi);
- encouraged children to use their home languages in the classroom;
- used their own languages in the classroom;
- developed positive attitudes towards language;
- learned and used basic words in children's home languages;
- invited families to the classroom to share stories in home languages;
- encouraged the use of the iTEO app at home;
- encouraged children to listen to iTEO stories in languages other than Luxembourgish;
- modelled languages;
- fostered language awareness;
- promoted multilingualism; and
- designed digital language-learning activities that allowed for peer-grouping.

Multilingual classrooms are better!

The iTEO study clearly showed that multilingual classrooms work better than monolingual ones. When given the opportunity and the freedom, bilingual children naturally translanguaged. They used their entire language toolbox to communicate effectively, manage the school language and take control of their learning.

> 'The children felt much freer when they realized that the use of a language other than Luxembourgish was accepted.'

Claudine concluded that when classrooms are open to home languages everyone wins: children collaborate and learn, teachers connect with children in new ways, and families participate in the classroom agenda.

LAP School Profile 7: From Swedish-only to Swedish-plus

Anita Isaksson and Anneli Wessman

Immigration in Sweden

In size and population, Sweden is the largest of the five Nordic countries (Norway, Iceland, Finland, Sweden and Denmark). It has a population of approximately 10 million and has been a member of the European Union (EU) since 1995. After WWII, Sweden became a land of immigration. Most immigration in the 1950s and 1960s was from neighbouring Nordic countries, with the largest numbers coming from Finland. Since the early 1970s, immigration has consisted mainly of refugee migration and family reunification from non-European countries in the Middle East and Latin America. In the 1990s Sweden received thousands of refugees from the former Yugoslavia. By 2000, immigrants had become a significant part of Swedish society. Most were born outside the EU. Recent immigrants to Sweden come from Syria and the African countries of Eritrea and Somalia. The proportion of people in Sweden with a non-Swedish background is currently approaching one-third of the population.[11]

Green Road School

Green Road School (hereafter GRS) is a highly diverse compulsory public school located in a suburban town in central Sweden. In 2015, enrolment at GRS stood at 355 and included three preschool groups (aged five to six) and 16 Grade 1–6 classrooms (aged seven to 12).

Since 2007, the number of newcomer students attending GRS and neighbouring schools has increased significantly. The majority of these newcomers are families who emigrated from the Middle East (Iraq, Iran, Turkey and Syria) and East Africa (Somalia, Kenya and Ethiopia). Many of the newcomer parents are unemployed, while others work at low-paying, low-status jobs such as bus drivers, restaurant workers and cleaners. In 2015, 21% of the children attending GRS spoke Swedish at home, while 79% had a home language other than Swedish. Of the 14 different non-Swedish home languages, Somali (53%) and Kurdish (16%) were the most numerous. Other home languages included Albanian, Arabic, Bosnian, Chinese, Dari, English, Finnish, Pashto, Romany, Russian, Dari and Tigrinya.

The GRS teachers have extensive experience, and many have worked at the school for more than 10 years. In addition to Swedish, some speak the following nine languages: Finnish, Somali, Kurdish, Turkish, Arabic, English, German, French and Albanian.

Support for newcomer students

Teachers in Sweden's preschools and compulsory schools are required to include newcomers in mainstream classrooms and support their mother tongues or home languages. The 'Mother tongue tuition' chapter in the 2011 National Agency of Education curriculum document requires teachers to provide newcomers with opportunities to '... develop their cultural identity and become multilingual' (Skolverket, 2011: 83).

'Teaching in the mother tongue should aim at helping the pupils to develop knowledge in and about the mother tongue.

Teaching should stimulate the pupils' interest in reading and writing in their mother tongue.

The teaching should help the pupils to master their knowledge of the structure of the mother tongue and become conscious of its importance for their own learning in different school subjects.'

The Mother Tongue Syllabus lists grade-level 'core content', including specific mother-tongue (MT) skills such as listening and speaking, reading and writing, narrative and non-fiction texts, use of language and culture and identity. Grade-level 'knowledge requirements' include the development of home language conversation and literacy ability and the comparison of the home and school (Swedish) language. Since mid-2016, all newcomers between the ages of seven and 16 are required by a directive from the Swedish School Board to go through a 'knowledge assessment evaluation' interview. At this time, home languages, prior schooling, experiences, interests and Swedish school requirements are discussed. The level of newcomers' subject knowledge is also assessed, and samples of home language literacy ability and numeracy skills are evaluated.

Guided by policy and school board directives, GRS has four support programmes for newcomers:

- Three MT teachers (two Somali and one Kurdish) conduct weekly 40- to 60-minute home language lessons with newcomer students during or after school. Following the Mother Tongue Syllabus described earlier, the MT teachers work in collaboration with the classroom and the Swedish as a second language (SSL) teachers.
- Five SSL teachers work in collaboration with classroom and subject teachers both in the classroom and on a withdrawal basis.
- MT study tutors support the academic work of newcomer students before, during or after class time.
- 'Buddies' are classmates who speak the newcomers' home languages. They help their newly arrived classmates navigate the new school and manage schoolwork.

The GRS multilingual journey

In 2007, under the leadership of Anita, the principal, the GRS teachers started moving towards inclusive instructional practice. They gradually abandoned monolingual or Swedish-only teaching, embraced a multilingual, Swedish-plus approach, included home languages in the school agenda and created spaces for the voices of newcomers. Using LAP12, they implemented multilingual activities and created a multilingual school language policy. They engaged in professional discussions, collaborated with university researchers and extended their knowledge about multilingualism by attending meetings and courses.

Since 2013, GRS has been involved in two international projects, collaborating with teachers in Canada and the UK – countries with high numbers of newcomers and highly successful multilingual teaching programmes. These collaborations were initiated by Anneli, an SSL teacher and Anita, the school principal, and were part of a 'long-term process of change'. They have helped the teachers of GRS and neighbouring schools extend and sustain their multilingual practice and help newcomer students participate in the curriculum and succeed in school. Of the many LAP actions implemented by Anneli, three are described here.

Action 1: Who are you?

This activity started with the question: 'Who are you?' Using a world map, Anneli shared her own immigration story with the children. She then invited the newcomers to locate their countries of origin or birth, share immigration experiences and discuss their names and home languages. Using their 'strongest' language, the children prepared 'identity frames' that included photos and personal information. Using pieces of red thread, the frames were matched to the newcomers' countries of origin. The heading 'World Map' was translated into five languages and added to the top of the display (Figure 3.21). Newcomers presented their identity frames to the class. In many cases, the presentations were in home languages, with Swedish interpretation provided by classmates. New arrivals were invited to add their identity frames to the display, making this an ongoing activity.

Action 2: Dual-language story writing

To start this activity, Anneli informed families that the children would be engaged in dual-language story writing (Figure 3.22). The children were asked to choose a topic and write about it, using their home language and, if possible, Swedish. Families were

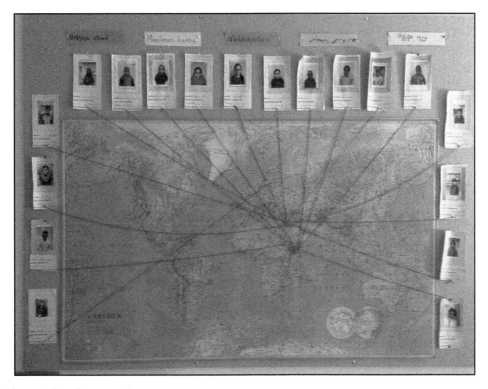

Figure 3.21 Who are you?

Figure 3.22 A dual-language book

asked to support this initiative by helping their children. Using technological tools such as electronic translators and the examples in the Thornwood Dual Language Showcase, a library of student-prepared dual-language books,[12] the GRS teachers encouraged the newcomers to work together and share ideas.

As the activity proceeded, Anneli noted the following:

- Newcomers were curious about each other's languages, asked questions and shared information about words and phrases. Children from different language backgrounds worked together.
- The initial anxieties and uncertainties of some children turned into engagement, followed by success. For example, one child who described the activity as 'too hard' completed a dual-language book and read it out loud in both his home language and in Swedish, to the applause and cheers of his classmates and teachers.
- Some children prepared folk tales or stories they heard at home and were anxious to share with their teacher and classmates.
- Classmates, parents and MT tutors helped those who had difficulty writing their stories in their home languages.
- Children were proud of their story writing and happily shared their work. One child was so proud of her story that she read it over the phone to her grandmother in Somalia. When a dual-language book went home, one newcomer reported that: 'Everyone wanted to read it!'
- The dual-language storybooks were added to classroom libraries.
- Response from families was positive. For example, one parent came to school, shook the teacher's hand and said: 'Tack. Tvåspråkiga boken är mycket bra.' ('Thank you. The dual-language book is very good.')

- The Swedish children benefited from the dual-language activity. They were curious and interested in the languages of their classmates and expressed an interest in learning new languages.

Action 3: Language of the month

To begin a school-wide initiative called Månadens språk or Language of the Month, Anneli decided to take a different approach. She started with English rather than with a home language. Since English instruction begins in Grade 1, she felt that this was a familiar language for all GRS teachers and children. Language of the Month displays included photos, words and phrases and language facts. Anneli felt that it was also important to showcase languages with a small number of speakers. For example, she selected Tigrinya, a language spoken mainly in Eritrea and northern Ethiopia. The five children who helped prepare the display were enthusiastic and excited about showcasing their language.

Action 4: Geography, money, civics and languages

Picking up on the children's interest in the newly released Swedish krona banknotes and coins, Anneli planned an engaging, multilingual lesson, integrating maths, geography, citizenship education (civics) and literacy. Discussion topics included home country currencies, such as the Somali shilling and senti, earning and spending money ('To buy food at the market'), the value of various banknotes and coins, the identification of persons on banknotes and inscriptions on coins. With the help of two MT tutors (speakers of Somali and Arabic), children used their 'strongest' language to prepare a currency chart, where the new Swedish krona banknotes and coins were labelled in Swedish, Somali and Arabic. The chart (see Figure 3.23) was displayed in the school hall and shared with the GRS community.

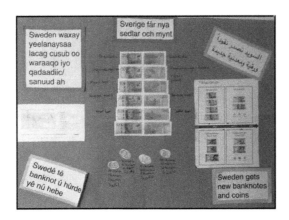

Figure 3.23 Currency chart

LAP in Specialized Programmes

(1) Preschool
(2) Language intervention
(3) English as a second language

The three LAP profiles presented here come from teachers working in English-medium specialized programmes in Canada.

LAP Programme Profile 1: Preschool

Angelpreet Singh

Background

The Westcoast Programme (hereafter referred to as WP) is a provincially funded, drop-in, early-learning initiative for young children (from birth to five) who do not attend out-of-home childcare. The WP is housed in a suburban public school with a highly diverse student population. For example, in the 2015–2016 school year over 50% of the students were identified as English language learners. The majority of the children attending WP were Punjabi-speaking.

Angelpreet, a doctoral candidate in the languages, cultures and literacies programme at a Canadian university, worked in the WP and provided the information for this profile. The WP is part of her larger study which looks at the language skills of young children growing up in Punjabi homes and the ways in which parents, grandparents, teachers and peers support their literacy learning.

The WP holds two daily sessions, five days per week. When this profile was prepared, over 60 children from mostly Punjabi- and Hindi-speaking families from India and Pakistan attended the programme. Other home languages of the families included Albanian, Arabic, Khmer, Tagalog and Urdu. Using a play-based curriculum, the programme strives to prepare preschool children for full-day kindergarten. During the half-day session, the children are encouraged to visit different learning centres (creative arts, daily living and blocks) and interact with their peers. Parents and grandparents are present and are encouraged to participate in the WP activities. The director of the WP (referred to here as GR) is an experienced early childhood educator who speaks English, Gujarati, Hindi and Urdu. Of the many multilingual actions GR implemented in the WP, three are described here.

Action 1: Open door language policy

'My goal is to include everyone in the program.'

GR

GR's classroom door is open to home languages. She encourages children and families to participate in the WP using their home languages. She uses Punjabi and Hindi to connect with non-English speaking children and families, to better understand them and learn how they support their young children's learning at home.

In the exchange that follows, GR is discussing a drawing created by a four-year-old child who speaks Punjabi and has limited proficiency in English. The grandmother is also present. While the child uses only Punjabi, GR speaks English and Punjabi. Following GR's opening question ('What did you make?'), the grandmother participates by asking questions in Punjabi:

GR:	What did you make?
Child:	Mera ghar. (My house.)
GR:	Tuhaada ghar bahut sohna hai. (Your house is very beautiful.)
Child:	Eh mere mama, eh mere papa, eh mere dadiji. (This is my mother, this is my father and this is my grandmother.)
Grandmother:	Eh ki hai? (What is this?)
Child:	Suraj. (Sun.)
GR:	Yes, you're right!
Child:	Drukhat. (Tree.)
Grandmother:	Eh ki hai? (What is this?)
Child:	Badal. (Clouds.)
GR:	I really like your drawing. Good job.

Action 2: Play is more than fun

When GR discovered that many Punjabi families believe that children's play is unrelated to learning, she engaged them in discussions about the developmental importance of children's play. She invited them to help create dual-language posters that showed the value of different aspects of children's play. The posters were displayed in the WP classroom and served as reminders of what really happens when children engage in play activities. For example, a Punjabi-English poster entitled 'When I build with blocks, I am learning to ...' listed the skills that children develop as they play with blocks: small muscle control, eye-hand coordination, maths concepts such as shapes, counting, sorting, thinking, problem solving, the use of imagination and interaction with peers. Overall, families were open to the new explanation of play. They started stepping back to allow their children to explore and discover.

Action 3: Early literacy

GR discovered that sharing books with children before bedtime was not a common practice among most Punjabi families. She also found that many of the parents and grandparents who were educated in India had very clear ideas about teaching young children to read and write. They believed, for example, that an adult-directed, structured, skill-based approach should be used and that children should be seated at tables completing worksheets. The reward for this 'school work' was free play. Some of the grandmothers attending the WP were concerned that worksheets were not provided and created their own by drawing lines on paper and encouraging their grandchildren to practise writing English letters, words and numbers (Figure 3.24).

In line with these structured views on literacy teaching, many families brought commercially prepared materials, such as English alphabet and number 'activity-sticker' books to the WP classroom. They encouraged children to complete the matching, tracing, practising and copying activities. In response to this, GR did four things:

- increased book-sharing;
- modelled book reading;
- acknowledged the literacy views of the families; and
- provided families with activity-based, child-centred literacy resources.

Book sharing

GR shared English-language books with children often and spontaneously. She invited families to participate in the daily story time, where stories were shared and where she modelled reading strategies, such as asking questions (both content and open-ended), focusing on story sequence, explaining words and key events, and encouraging children to recall story details and create word lists. Home languages were regularly used in the English-language book-sharing sessions. Translations were provided to help children and families understand words, concepts and storylines.

Sharing dual-language books is an important part of the WP literacy agenda. GR selects books that are culturally relevant to the families. For example, knowing that bread (or flatbread) baking was familiar to Punjabi families, she chose a dual-language (Punjabi-English) version of 'The Little Red Hen', a story about a hen who finds a

Figure 3.24 Creating a worksheet

grain of wheat and asks her farmyard friends to help her harvest, thresh, mill and bake bread.

In reading the dual-language book, GR adopted the one-page bilingual approach. After a parent or grandparent read a page in Punjabi, she read the same page in English. Children were delighted and proud when their parents or grandparents came into the classroom to participate in story time.

GR encouraged families to share books with their children at home and in the WP. She also invited children to explore books on their own and with their friends.

Your way – our way

GR acknowledged and respected the adult-directed teaching views held by many families by preparing activities that included both a structured and a creative component. For example, children were invited to engage in activities their own way, or follow the prescribed (colour, cut out, label and paste) instructions. GR explained the two options in English and in home languages and reported that some grandparents directed the activity, while others encouraged children to take the lead.

Literacy resources

GR provided families with a number of resources to help them engage children in literacy activities. For example, picture cards of familiar topics such as food, shopping, animals, nature, and toys with bilingual labels were sent home to be shared with children. Included with the cards were the same modelling strategies GR had demonstrated in the classroom. GR reported that response to her literacy engagement suggestions was positive. Families were grateful for the support and were willing to learn new ways to help their children learn and succeed.

LAP Programme Profile 2: Language Intervention

Allison Kennedy

Background

This profile reports on the adoption of LAP in an early language intervention programme (hereafter ELI) offered by the Toronto District School Board. ELI provides language and literacy support for five-year-old children who have moderate to significant delays in oral language comprehension (understanding) and language expression (speaking). For example, these children have been identified with one or more of the following primary language impairment concerns: limited proficiency in the home language; limited proficiency in English; small vocabulary; short sentence use; difficulty in understanding and following three-step directions; limited home literacy experiences; limited ability to retell stories; and challenges with social interaction. The ELI programme uses high interest stories, follow-up activities and repeated multimedia presentations to help children develop their language and literacy skills and gain confidence in speaking and sharing their ideas.

At the time of writing, 32 children, divided into four groups of eight, attended the ELI eight-month programme on a part-time basis: two half-days or six hours per week. For the remainder of the week, the children attended full-day kindergarten in a nearby 'feeder school'.

The ELI teaching team works closely with the kindergarten teachers and families. For example:

- interviews with parents are conducted at the beginning and end of the programme;
- consultation meetings with the teaching team take place throughout the programme period;
- a classroom blog and website update parents on classroom activities and provide suggestions for home language teaching; and
- progress reports are shared both with kindergarten teachers and parents.

At the time of the profile preparation, the ELI teaching team consisted of two professionals with more than 10 years of teaching experience: a kindergarten teacher and a speech and language pathologist. In the second half of the reporting period, a graduate student joined the ELI team for a part-time practicum. The profile that follows is based on observation notes prepared by the teaching team and the graduate student.

The children and families

The ELI classroom is housed in a large Toronto public school situated in a high-immigrant, high-density, low-income, high-unemployment area. While some of the parents are professionals, most are service and maintenance workers or are unemployed. In most of the families, mothers do not work outside the home.

Two-thirds (65%) of the children in the ELI classroom were born in Canada to newcomer parents. The remainder were born outside Canada, in Pakistan, Bangladesh, India, Libya, Syria, Vietnam and Iraq. Of the 15 different home languages reported by the parents, Urdu is spoken most often, followed by English and Gujarati (Table 3.1).

The home language situation of the children is varied. In some cases, two or more languages are spoken in the home. Many of the parents are learning English and some lack literacy skills in their home languages. Many believe that exposure to two languages is confusing to children. They use English to help their children 'prepare' for school and share only English books with them. Some children arrive in the ELI classroom lacking 'a solid foundation' in either their home language or in English.

Journey to LAP: From English-only to English-plus

Before adopting LAP, the ELI instruction team reported that they followed the Ontario Ministry of Education directive and referred to newcomer children as English

Table 3.1 Children's home languages

Home languages	Number of children
Urdu	11
English	7
Gujarati	4
Arabic	2
Bengali	2
Hindi	2
Dari	1
Greek	1
Kurdish	1
Pashto	1
Punjabi	1
Spanish	1
Telugu	1
Turkish	1
Vietnamese	1

language learners (ELLs). They acknowledged the importance of home languages and encouraged parents to use their home languages with their children. In the classroom, the ELI team focused on helping children improve their English. However, attendance at a multilingual workshop and the introduction to LAP steered the ELI team in a new teaching direction. After learning about childhood bilingualism and LAP, they started rethinking and retooling their practice. Here are four LAP actions implemented by the ELI teaching team.

Action 1: What's in a name?

The first step in retooling their practice and moving towards LAP was to replace the term English language learners, which identifies newcomer children primarily as learners of the classroom language. They started using 'emergent bilingual' (García, 2009) or 'bilingual learner', two terms that identify the dual-language reality, potential and ability of newcomer children.

Action 2: The language and literacy lives of newcomer children

In order to better understand their newcomers and to build more effectively on their language and literacy skills, the ELI teaching team extended the initial family interview. They asked parents to provide information on the following topics:

- home language use;
- child's home language skills: comparison with native speakers of the same age;
- child's exposure to English;
- child's dominant language;

- technology in the home: computers, tablets, games and movies;
- family literacy practices;
- child's experiences with print and books: familiarity, interest, public library visits;
- children's books in the home (number and languages);
- visits to the country of origin;
- language views: home language, English, bilingualism; and
- concerns about their child's language development and use.

Action 3: Engaging newcomer families

'We keep in close contact with our parents and keep them abreast of the stories, vocabulary and concepts we are working on and encourage them to work on these in their home language with their children.'

In order to engage newcomer families, the ELI team transformed the classroom blog into a multilingual, parent-friendly site. They added a translation feature and numerous links to multiliteracy websites and community resources. They also added the following four topics to their regular parent workshop schedule:

- the importance of home languages in children's overall development;
- the relationship between a strong home language and learning English;
- the advantages of bilingualism; and
- sharing dual-language books with children.

Parents were invited to the ELI classroom to observe the communication strategies that the teaching team used with the children. Three examples follow:

- Use of 'parallel talking' during activity centres, to build and elicit relevant vocabulary.
  For example: Teacher: 'Wow, you made a farm! I like that fence! That will keep all those sheep and cows from running away!'
- Giving child-friendly definitions of new words.
  For example: Teacher: 'You look exhausted! That means you look very, very tired.'
- Recasting and modelling grammatically correct sentences.
  For example: Child: 'She goed to store.' Teacher: 'That's true! She went to the store.'

Families were encouraged to use these strategies at home with their children. They were also invited to come to the classroom to help the children create multilingual signs and displays and to share books in their home languages. They were encouraged to follow up on classroom activities by providing their children with translations of new words and by reinforcing concepts introduced in the class. For example, after the children listened to a story called 'We're Going on a Bear Hunt', which included common prepositions of direction and position such as 'over, under, through, across', parents were encouraged to include these words into their everyday home language conversations with their children and to practise their use.

Action 4: Home languages in the ELI classroom

With the help of families, home languages became 'visible' in the ELI classroom. For example, children's names in their home languages were added to library envelopes (Figure 3.25), a multilingual HELLO sign was posted on the classroom door, bilingual name cards were created and a multilingual songbook was compiled and shared with families. The ELI teaching team talked about the multilingual displays with the children and provided the English names of home languages ('You speak Pashto at home.').

Your home language is important

In group discussions and in one-on-one conversations, the ELI teachers reminded children that all languages are important and that knowing more than one language is a good thing. They invited the children to use their home languages with each other in the classroom. They also asked the children to provide home language translations ('How do you say that in your language?') for single words and concepts.

Figure 3.25 Bilingual library envelopes

Child:	You buy it with dinar.
Teacher:	What is dinar?
Child:	(Shrugs)
Teacher:	Is that money in your language, in Kurdish?
Child:	(Looks at teacher with bright eyes.)
Teacher:	Dinar, am I saying it right?
Child:	(Smiles, nods in agreement.)
Teacher:	(Turns to a Spanish-speaking child) how do you say 'money' in Spanish?
Child:	(Excited) Dinero.
Teacher:	Ah, dinero.

The ELI teaching team reported the following responses to LAP actions in the classroom:

- Initially children were unsure about using their home languages in the classroom. Invitations such as 'How do you say that in your home language?' were often met with confusion and silence. Yet, with time, children reached a 'comfort zone' and home languages became a natural and accepted part of classroom conversations.
- Children became aware of each other's home languages. They used home languages with each other, and helped one another. For example, when a child did not respond to the teacher's question, a classmate stepped in and said: 'The same for you, you are Pakistan.'
- Children were excited and proud when their home languages were used in classroom discussions.
- Quiet children seemed to 'wake up' and were more attentive when asked to use their home language.
- Improved ability in home language use was noted, especially in vocabulary size.

LAP Programme Profile 3: English as a Second Language

Safiya Shere and Reena Soin

More and more English as a second language teachers in Canadian schools are adopting LAP in their work with newcomers. This means that in teaching the school language, they acknowledge, scaffold and build on newcomers' prior language knowledge and skills. In so doing, they help these children learn the school language, join the curriculum and grow bilingually.

The four LAP actions presented here come from Safiya and Reema, two Canadian ESL teachers. The children in their classrooms are at different stages in their English language learning.

Figure 3.26 A special moment with my mother

Action 1: My mother

In this activity, Safiya's seven-year-old Arabic-speaking newcomers were invited to talk about special moments they have shared with their mothers (Figure 3.26). Safiya introduced the activity with visuals and talked about her own mother. She used simple sentences, repeated key words and pointed to specific parts of the visuals. Interest was high as children 'chimed in', labelled the visuals, used their home languages and attempted to use words in English.

Safiya then asked the children to draw a picture of a special moment they had shared with their mothers. To ensure that the instructions were understood, she asked a bilingual speaker of Arabic to explain the task to classmates. As the children drew pictures and chatted in Arabic, Safiya asked questions about their work, provided relevant words and phrases and encouraged them to repeat what she said. She described the activity as engaging because the topic was meaningful and relevant. Also it provided the newcomers with the opportunity to use their home language and learn English words and phrases.

Action 2: Comparing languages

Safiya encouraged newcomers to make connections between Arabic and English (Figure 3.27). Here are the topics she discussed with the children:

- language families;
- English names of languages;
- speech sounds of Arabic and English;

Figure 3.27 Comparing Arabic and English

- writing systems;
- singular and plural forms;
- basic verb tenses (present, past, future);
- text directionality; and
- words that start with the same sound(s) in English and Arabic.

Action 3: Watching, listening, reading, sharing and writing

In order to engage the newcomers in narrative writing, Safiya used an Arabic-language video of a familiar story (Little Red Riding Hood), with English subtitles (Figure 3.28; see https://www.youtube.com/watch?v=XLlHaLChWAQ). As the video played, Arabic-speaking newcomers watched and listened, while their Arabic-English bilingual classmates read the English subtitles. Safiya then used screenshots to explore and discuss story characters, setting, plot and sequence. The children's task was to think of adjectives to describe the story characters. The children worked together and created bilingual adjective charts using Arabic and English (Figure 3.29).

Figure 3.28 Subtitled Little Red Riding Hood

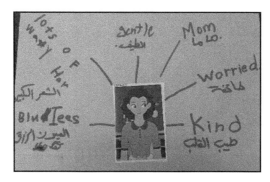

Figure 3.29 Bilingual adjective list

Action 4: Preparing for the Terry Fox Run

Terry Fox was a Canadian athlete and cancer research activist. In 1980, when he was diagnosed with bone cancer and had his right leg amputated, he embarked on an east-to-west, cross-Canada run to raise money for cancer research. After 143 days and 5373 km, Terry was forced to stop running because cancer had appeared in his lungs. He died in 1981, at the age of 22. The Terry Fox Run is an annual event in many Canadian schools.

Reema decided to prepare the newcomers for the school-wide Terry Fox Run. She provided multilingual electronic resources (keyboards, books, videos and photos) and engaged the children in discussions about athletes, heroes and the life of Terry Fox. Children worked together to complete worksheets (Figures 3.30 and 3.31), in the language(s) of their choice.

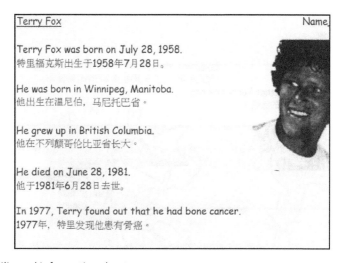

Figure 3.30 Bilingual information sheet

Draw a picture of yourself doing something with your hero.
画一个你自己做的事情与你的英雄的照片。

Figure 3.31 Playing basketball with my hero

Consider this …

(1) Using Table 3.1 (Home languages in the classroom) as a guide, think about the different ways home languages appear in your classroom and in your school: Are they seen? Are they heard? Are they used? Are they included in the curriculum?

(2) Create a pie chart of the languages represented in your classroom and also in your school. Here is a link to easy graph preparation: https://nces.ed.gov/nceskids/graphing/classic/.

(3) Of the many LAP actions described in the profiles, list the ones that could work in your classroom, in your programme or in your school. Think of ways to adapt and modify the actions to meet your context.

(4) How is linguistic diversity addressed in the policy and curriculum documents of your country or school region? Do the directives provide guidelines, resources and support for multilingual teaching? How can you get involved in updating these documents?

(5) Think about your own multilingual teaching journey. When did you first learn about multilingual teaching? What was your initial response? How has your multilingual teaching evolved and changed?

Notes

(1) The Canadian Museum of Immigration at Pier 21: https://www.youtube.com/watch?v=1_yFP71p53k (accessed 18 December 2017).
(2) See http://community.smu.ca/atlantic/documents/NS_Report_Final_Nov_29.pdf (accessed 18 December 2017).
(3) See https://studentservices.ednet.ns.ca/sites/default/files/esl_guidelines_web.pdf (accessed 18 December 2017).
(4) These teachers worked in kindergarten and Grades, 1, 2, 3, 4 and 5.
(5) http://schools.peelschools.org/1363/DualLanguage/Documents/index.htm (accessed 18 December 2017).
(6) Canadians recognize Remembrance Day, originally called Armistice Day, every 11 November. This day marks the end of hostilities during WWI and provides an opportunity to recall all those who have served in the nation's defence.
(7) A hypocorism, also known as a pet name or calling name, is a shorter, diminutive or augmentative form of a word or given name: for example, Billy, from William, and Peggy, from Elizabeth.
(8) See http://www.childs-play.com/teacher-zone/what_is_a_storyshack.html (accessed 18 December 2017).
(9) See https://en.wikipedia.org/wiki/Languages_of_Luxembourg (accessed 18 December 2017).
(10) See https://iteo.uni.lu (accessed 18 December 2017).
(11) See https://en.wikipedia.org/wiki/Immigration_to_Sweden (accessed 18 December 2017).
(12) See http://schools.peelschools.org/1363/DualLanguage/Documents/index.htm (accessed 18 December 2017).

References

Ada, A.F. and Campoy, I. (2003) *Authors in the Classroom: A Transformative Education Process*. New York: Pearson.
Arnbjörnsdóttir, B. (2008) Tvítyngi, annað mál, erlent mál. *Málfríður* 24 (1), 17–23.
Arnbjörnsdóttir, B. (2010) Skólar og fjölskyldur sem málsamfélög. In H. Ragnarsdóttir and E.S. Jónsdóttir (eds) *Fjölmenning og skólastarf* (pp. 315–336). Reykjavik: Rannsóknarstofa í fjölmenningarfræðum, KHÍ og Háskólaútgáfan.
Ashworth, M. (1998) *Blessed with Bilingual Brains*. Vancouver: Pacific Educational.
Bernhard, J.K., Cummins, J., Campoy, I., Ada, A., Winsler, A. and Bleiker, C. (2006) Identity texts and literacy development among preschool English language learners: Enhancing learning opportunities for children at risk of learning disabilities. *Teachers College Record* 108 (11), 2380–2405.
Bernhard, J.K., Winsler, A., Bleiker, C., Ginieniewicz, J. and Madigan, A. (2008) Read my story: Promoting early literacy among diverse, urban, preschool children in poverty with the Early Authors Program. *Journal of Education for Students Placed at Risk* 13 (1), 76–105.
Chumak-Horbatsch, R. (2012) *Linguistically Appropriate Practice: A Guide for Working with Young Immigrant Children*. Toronto: University of Toronto Press.
CMAS (2015) *Caring for Syrian Refugee Children*. See https://cmascanada.ca/supporting-refugees/.
Cummins, J. (2018) Multilingualism in the classroom: 'I think it's helping my brain grow'. *Scottish Language Review* 33. doi:10.6084/m9.figshare.5925088
Cummins, J. and Early, M. (eds) (2011) *Identity Texts: The Collaborative Creation of Power in Multilingual Schools*. Stoke-on-Trent: Trentham Books.
Cummins, J. and Persad, R. (2014) Teaching through a multilingual lens: The evolution of EAL policy and practice in Canada. *Education Matters* 2, 3–40.
García, O. (2009) Emergent bilinguals and TESOL: What's in a name? *TESOL Quarterly* 43 (2), 322–326. Special issue edited by Shelley Taylor.
García, O. and Li Wei (2014) *Translanguaging: Language, Bilingualism, and Education*. London: Palgrave Macmillan.

Gunnþórsdóttir, H., Barill, S. and Meckl, M. (in press) Diversity and multiculturalism in Icelandic schools: Parents' and teachers' voices. *Nordic Studies on Diversity in Education.*

Hagstofa Íslands (2015) *Börn í leikskólum með erlent móðurmál 1998–2017 [Children in Pre-primary Schools with Foreign Mother Tongue 1998–2017].* See http://px.hagstofa.is/pxis/pxweb/is/Samfelag/ Samfelag__skolamal__1_leikskolastig__0_lsNemendur/SKO01103.px/?rxid=b0957a0f-5b74-40fb-b987-747deb5e89f6.

Hjartardottir, G. (2013) *Lesið í leik: Læsisstefna leikskóla.* Reykjavik: Skóla- og frístundasvið Reykjavíkur. See http://issuu.com/skola_og_fristundasvid/docs/l__sisstefna_tilbu__i__2.

Icelandic Government (2009) *Niðurstöður Pisa rannsóknarinnar.* Reykjavik: Námsmatsstofnun. See https://www.menntamalaraduneyti.is/frettir/Frettatilkynningar/nr/5792.

Icelandic Ministry of Education, Science and Culture (2011) *National Curriculum Guide for Preschools.* Reykjavik: Mennta- og menningarmálaráðuneytið.

Icelandic Parliament (2008) *Lög um leikskóla No. 90/2008 [Icelandic Preschool Act].* Reykjavik: Alþingi. See http://www.althingi.is/lagas/136b/2008090.html.

Icelandic Parliament (2015) *Tillaga til þingsályktunar um framkvæmdaáætlun í málefnum innflytjenda fyrir árin 2016–2019.* Reykjavik: Alþingi. See http://www.althingi.is/altext/pdf/145/s/1285.pdf.

Íslensk Málnefnd (2013) *Ályktun um stöðu íslenskrar tungu 2013.* Reykjavik: Íslensk Málnefnd. See http:// www.islenskan.is/images/Alyktanir-pdf/alyktun_IM_2013.pdf.

Jónsdóttir, F.B. (2011) Allt sem þú þorir ekki að tala um verða fordómar seinna meir: Rýnt í hlutverk leikskólakennara með fjölbreyttum barnahópi. Unpublished MEd thesis, Menntavísindasvið Háskóla Íslands [Iceland College of Education].

Jónsson, A.K. (2013) *Tölfræðilegar upplýsingar um erlenda ríkisborgara og innflytjendur á Íslandi.* Ísafjörður: Fjölmenningarsetur.

Kirsch, C. (2018) Young children capitalising on their entire language repertoire for language learning at school. *Language, Culture and Curriculum* 31 (1), 39–55.

Kirsch, C. and Bes, A. (2019) Emergent multilinguals learning languages with the iPad app iTEO: A study in primary schools in Luxembourg. *Language Learning* 47 (2), 204-218.

Leclerc, J. (2008) Luxembourg. In *L'aménagement linguistique dans le monde.* Quebec: TLFQ Université.

Moll, L.C., Amanti, C., Neff, D. and González, N. (1992) Funds of knowledge for teaching: Using a qualitative approach to connect homes and classrooms. *Theory into Practice* 31 (2), 132–141.

Ólafsdóttir, S. (2010) Íslenskur orðaforði íslenskra grunnskólanema sem eiga annað móðurmál en íslensku. Unpublished MA thesis, Menntavísindasvið Háskóla Íslands [Iceland College of Education].

Ólafsdóttir, S. (2015) The development of vocabulary and reading comprehension among Icelandic second language learners. Unpublished doctoral thesis, Menntavísindasvið Háskóla Íslands [Iceland College of Education].

Ragnarsdóttir, Hr. (2015) *Málþroski leikskólabarna, Orðaspjall. Að efla orðaforða og hlustunarskilning barna með bóklestri.* Reykjanesbær: Leikskólinn Tjarnarsel.

Reykavík City Department of Education and Youth (2014) *The World is Here: Reykjavik City Department of Education and Youth Policy on Multicultural Education and Leisure.* Reykjavik: Reykavík City Department of Education and Youth. See https://reykjavik.is/sites/default/files/fjolmenningarstefna_ uppsett_enska_n_2.pdf.

Reykjavíkurborg (2015) *Skýrsla starfshóps um móðurmálskennslu barna með annað móðurmál en íslensku.* Reykjavik: Skóla- og frístundasvið Reykjavíkur. See http://reykjavik.is/sites/default/files/skjol_ borgarstjornarfundur/lokaskyrsla_starfshops_um_modurmalskennslu.pdf.

Reykjavíkurborg (2016) *Stefna og starfsáætlun skóla- og frístundasviðs Reykjavíkur.* Reykjavik: Skóla- og frístundasvið Reykjavíkur. See http://reykjavik.is/sites/default/files/starfsaaetlun_sfs_2016_loka_ heild.pdf.

Scardamalia, M. (2002) Collective cognitive responsibility for the advancement of knowledge. In B. Smith (ed.) *Liberal Education in a Knowledge Society* (pp. 67–98). Chicago, IL: Open Court.

Schecter, S. and Cummins, J. (eds) (2003) *Multilingual Education in Practice: Using Diversity as a Resource.* Portsmouth, NH: Heinemann.

Skolverket (2011) *Curriculum for the Compulsory School, Preschool Class and the Recreation Centre, 2011.* Stockholm: Skolverket.

Þórðardóttir, Þ. (2012) Menningarlæsi: hlutverk barnaefnis í uppeldi og menntun telpna og drengja í tveimur leikskólum. Unpublished doctoral thesis, Reykjavik: Menntavísindasvið Háskóla Íslands [Iceland College of Education].

Weber, J.J. and Horner, K. (2008) The language situation in Luxembourg. *Current Issues in Language Planning* 9 (1), 69–128.

4 LAP Challenges

LAP teachers reported a number of challenges that emerged in their multilingual teaching. For example, they noticed that some children were disengaged during LAP activities. They also wondered why newcomers hesitated to use their home languages when invited to do so. They asked for guidance on how to best support single speakers of little-known languages and how to bring families into their multilingual agendas. In this chapter, we turn our attention to these four challenges and discuss possible solutions.

Challenge 1: Engaging Monolingual and Bilingual Children

A number of LAP teachers reported that attention to newcomers and their home languages at times overshadowed monolingual and bilingual children, leaving them disengaged during LAP activities and discussions. Here are three examples:

- Following a discussion about home languages, a five-year-old monolingual child tearfully said: 'I have no language.'
- Class discussions about food, clothing and cultural artefacts excluded monolingual children, who said that they have little or nothing to contribute.
- Lists of home languages created by the class often *omitted* the school language.

(?) How can the LAP teacher include everyone in discussions and activities?

Here are four strategies to ensure that all children are included in LAP discussions and activities.

Strategy 1: Don't forget the school language

Be sure to include the school language in class language lists, charts and displays. Also, add other official languages: for example, French in Canadian English-medium schools. Remind monolingual children that their mastery of the school language is important. Introduce them to language enrichment resources such as a thesaurus (a book that lists synonyms) and books of idioms. These will help them extend and enrich their speaking and writing skills.

Strategy 2: Language buddies

Set aside time for 'language buddies', a time for children to work in self-selected pairs (or small groups) to share languages and learn from each other. Provide resources such as picture dictionaries, YouTube clips and picture cards to generate discussion about language features, similarities and differences, pronunciation, writing systems and text directionality. Ask the children to share their language discoveries with the class.

Strategy 3: Language events

Many LAP teachers organize class and school-wide events where invited guests share information about home languages (see Helen's LAP profile). At these events, often called 'Mother Language Days' or 'Our Languages', speakers present the highlights of their home language and explain where it is spoken, the number of speakers worldwide, pronunciation, writing system and text directionality. Surprisingly, the school language is often excluded from these events.

Begin your language events with the school language. Make this a class project, guide the planning, provide resources, engage all children and invite the monolinguals to take the lead and share information about the school language. Recall how Tobin (Chapter 2) encouraged Matt to explore the variations of English and present his finding to his classmates.

Strategy 4: Add a language!
Saga Stephenson

Encourage monolingual children to learn words in a language spoken by a classmate. Here is an example from Saga's linguistically diverse preschool in Miðborg, Iceland.

About half of the children attending the Miðborg preschool do not speak Icelandic at home. In response to this diversity, the teachers launched two multilingual initiatives. The first one, the 'Töfrandi tungumál' or 'Magical languages', ensured that children's home languages were included in daily class activities. In the second initiative, 'Tungumál vikunnar' or 'Home language week', children's home languages were explored, compared and showcased.

Response to these multilingual initiatives was positive. Icelandic and newcomer families participated in the activities and encouraged their children to learn words in the languages of their friends. The dual-language list you see in Figure 4.1 was created by an Icelandic-speaking child and his father as a weekend project. It includes basic

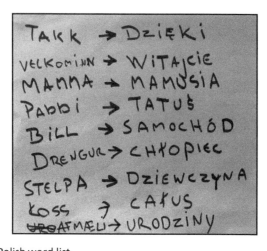

Figure 4.1 Icelandic-Polish word list

words (thanks, hello, mother, father, car, boy, girl, kiss, birthday) in Icelandic (on the left) and in Polish (on the right). Once completed, the list was shared with the class.

Challenge 2: Unwillingness to Use the Home Language

The profiles presented in the previous chapter show the dynamic presence of home languages in classrooms and children's positive and enthusiastic response to LAP. Yet teachers reported that both newcomer and bilingual children were often hesitant and unwilling to use their home language when invited and encouraged to do so. Others provided responses that LAP teachers described as 'surprising'.

In this section, we explore children's unwillingness to respond to teachers' language invitations. The explanations will help you understand why some bilingual and newcomer children hesitate to use their home languages in the classroom. The explanations, strategies and suggestions will help you understand these behaviours.

Say it in your home language!

LAP teachers use two different directives to encourage children to use their home languages: they ask questions and use commands. These directives are often met with looks of confusion, surprise uncertainty, and even anxiety.

Questions	Commands
'Do you speak Mandarin?'	'Talk the way you do at home.'
'How do you say ___ in your language?'	'You can speak Urdu here.'
'Can you translate that into your language?'	'Talk in your home language.'
'Do you use English at home?'	'Tell me in your own language.'

In response to these invitations, some children remain silent while others respond in the following ways:

- (Close to tears) 'I don't have a language.'
- 'I speak regular.'
- 'I talk like this' (produces gibberish sounds).
- 'I speak normal like this.'
- (Pointing to a classmate) 'I talk like him.'
- A five-year old newcomer: 'English … my home.' The teacher understood this as 'I use English at home', which was not the case.
- A six-year-old monolingual English speaker identified Arabic as 'my language', saying 'I'm Arabic, too', which was not true.
- In response to the question 'How do you say *orange* in Tamil?', an eight-year-old Tamil-speaking child responded 'orange'.

 ## Why do children respond with confusion and silence?

To answer this question, let's look at three things:

- young children's incomplete understanding of language concepts;
- parental teaching; and
- the words teachers use.

Young children's incomplete understanding of abstract language concepts

Children do not understand what is expected of them when teachers ask them to 'use' their home language. Why is this so? The answer is quite straightforward: because their understanding of abstract concepts such as language, language use, language identification, language ownership and language context is incomplete.

For example, all young children – not only newcomers and bilinguals – have an incomplete understanding of the following basic facts about language:

- that they are speakers of or that they 'use' or 'speak' a language;
- that they own or 'have' a language; and
- that one's language is a personal identity marker.

Also, when asked about their home language, they often mistakenly identify with the language of a classmate or the language under discussion.

Parental teaching

The invitation from teachers to use home languages in the classroom stands in contrast to what many newcomer and bilingual children hear at home. For example, a Grade 2 bilingual child responded to his teacher's invitation to speak Urdu in a Toronto classroom by saying:

'You need to talk English in school, my mom and dad says this.'
'You can't say Urdu in school.'

Other examples come from Canadian schoolyards, where mothers tell their children entering the school in the morning: 'Speak English', 'Only English here'.

Teachers' words

The words teachers use to invite children to use their home language are full of unknowns and are confusing to young children. Here are four examples:

- Words and phrases such as 'language', 'my language', 'your language', 'speak', 'tell' and 'talk' are confusing to young children generally, not only to newcomers and bilinguals.
- The phrase 'at home' and 'in your house' can have more than one meaning. It can refer to the place where the child lives, to the home of grandparents, babysitters or relatives, to the separate homes of mum and dad, or to the country of origin. The use of different languages in these places can make it difficult for children to connect language and place.
- Asking young newcomers to 'translate' from their home languages (which are not fully developed) into the school language (which they are learning) is beyond their cognitive and communicative abilities. An additional problem is using the word 'translate', which means providing a *written* equivalent, instead of 'interpret', which refers to *orally* putting ideas presented in one language into another.
- Most children do not know the names of their home languages. For example, a child who speaks *Deutsch* at home does not know that her language is called *German* in English. In the same way, a child who speaks *по українськи* does not know that the English name of her language is *Ukrainian*.

(?) How can teachers help young children understand language concepts?

Here are three strategies to help young children better understand abstract language concepts:

- talk about language;
- share books about language; and
- directly teach language concepts.

Strategy 1: Talk about language

Talk to children about language. Use the language factsheet that follows as a guide. In an age-appropriate way, tell them:

- that they are language users or speakers;
- that speakers of two languages are called bilinguals; and
- about your languages.

Language fact sheet

- Children can talk – adults can talk. Animals and babies can't.
- Animals communicate a limited number of messages.
- Apes and bonobo monkeys have been taught human sign languages.
- Young children will find gorilla communication fascinating. See the website Koko Kid's Club for information about gorilla habits and abilities: http://www.koko.org/kidsclub/learn/10facts.html.
- Languages have names.
- Our languages are spoken in different countries.
- Like people, languages belong to families.
- English, Spanish and French belong to the Indo-European language family.
- There are more than 6500 languages spoken in the world today.
- Languages are believed to have originated from one mother tongue.
- The most widely spoken language in the world is Mandarin.
- The Philippines has more than 1000 regional dialects and two official languages.
- More than 1000 different languages are spoken on the continent of Africa.
- Words that describe a particular cultural practice or idea do not translate precisely into another language.
- In nearly every language around the world, the word for 'mother' begins with an M sound.
- The following body parts allow us to speak: tongue, lips, larynx or voice box and vocal folds.
- To produce a word, about 100 muscles of the chest, neck, jaw, tongue and lips must work together.
- Each spoken word or short phrase is accompanied by its own pattern of muscular movements.
- All the information necessary for speaking is stored in the speech area of the brain.
- Early humans probably had a rudimentary speech system resembling animal communication.
- The first symbolic language emerged 2.5 million years ago, when early humans created tools.
- The brain has a 'critical period', a time when it acquires speech. If language is not acquired at this time, the child will not acquire speech later on.

? 'How many languages are there in the world?'

The Linguistic Society of America has an interesting page called 'How many languages are there in the world?', which can be shared with children. See: https://www.linguisticsociety.org/content/how-many-languages-are-there-world.

Strategy 2: Share books about language

Add language information books to your school and classroom libraries. Share them with children and make them available for personal and group discovery. Begin with *Chitchat: Celebrating the World's Languages* (see summary in the box). The child-friendly text and brightly coloured illustrations in this book will help children better understand language concepts, practices and behaviours. Lists of dual-language books and books about language can be found in the next chapter.

Jude, I. (2013) *Chitchat: Celebrating the World's Languages.* **Toronto: Kids Can Press.**

From: https://www.amazon.ca/Chitchat-Celebrating-Languages-Jude-Isabella/dp/1554537878

Award-winning children's science writer Jude Isabella has compiled everything a young reader would ever want to know about language into one accessible, visually stunning book. In lively text, both spoken and written language are explored, including: a basic history of human's use of language; how individuals learn language as babies; how writing systems and alphabets differ; the many sources and uses of slang; how languages evolved in different parts of the world; and why some languages became extinct.

More than 50 world languages are highlighted and children are offered opportunities to try out some phrases. Each separate topic is covered on a two-page spread, making the content manageable and approachable, and each spread is enhanced with bite-size sidebars that relate to or expand upon the information presented. With the strong focus on understanding and comparing cultures in today's social studies curricula, this book about languages throughout the world offers an interesting and unique way to do that. Simple activities suitable for individuals or groups appear throughout the book. This book includes essential reference tools, including a table of contents, a glossary and an index.

Strategy 3: Directly teach about language

Explicit or direct teaching is an effective way to help young children understand abstract language concepts. The three examples below come from LAP teachers who directly explained language concepts, introduced language terminology and taught children the English names of their home languages.

Example 1: Home language chart

In this example, a Grade 1 teacher in an English-language school used the home language chart (Table 4.1) to teach children language terminology and the English names of their languages. Following the chart, you will see how she explained language concepts to the children.

Table 4.1 Grade 1 Home language chart

Home languages	Number of speakers	Names of speakers
English	3	Miss Ross, Joshua, Elizabeth
Mandarin	4	Huan, Lin, Shan, Miss Pearl
Arabic	3	Amira, Baraka, Akbar
Urdu	3	Sabirah, Johara, Tahir
Polish	1	Agnieszka
Farsi	5	Ali, Sadri, Karim, Azin, Navid

LAP teacher's explanation of Table 4.1

Here's a chart that shows how we talk at home.
You can see three columns.

The first column lists six languages.
Let's count them to make sure there are six.
The languages are: English, Mandarin, Arabic, Urdu, Polish and Farsi.
Let's read the names of the languages together.
The second column shows the number of people who speak each language at home.
And the last column shows the names of the people who speak each language.

Let's have a closer look and start at the top:
Three people speak English at home: they are Miss Ross, Joshua and Elizabeth

Let's move on to other languages:
Four people speak Mandarin at home: they are Huan, Lin, Shan and Miss Pearl.
Three people speak Arabic: they are Amira, Baraka and Akbar.
Continues down the list, inviting the children to participate

Let's go back to English.
English is our school language.
English is the language used in Canada.
French is also used in Canada. You will learn French in school later.

We are all speakers of English.
And we are also speakers of other languages.
Some of us are learning English and some of us speak English at home.

Example 2: Understanding language concepts
Helen Arnold

When asked about explicit teaching, Helen, a kindergarten teacher, reported that she helps children understand language concepts in the following ways:

- using maps and globes to point out the countries where home languages are spoken;
- talking about the many different ways people speak and write;
- sharing her own languages with children: 'I speak English and German. I also know some words in Japanese.'
- providing vocabulary to help children articulate their language ideas, observations and feelings;
- creating a list of language-related words; and
- modelling the correct use of language terms, e.g.: **Child**: I'm Korea.

    Helen: Yes, you're Korean.

Example 3: Bilingual name cards

In this example, a Grade 2 teacher used a bilingual name card to teach language concepts:

- Dhruv has a home language (Hindi) that is different from the school language (English);
- Dhruv is bilingual or a speaker of two languages;
- the English name of Dhruv's language is Hindi;
- Dhruv comes from India; and
- Dhruv's name means 'northern star'.

Dhruv	ध्रुव

Children's response to direct teaching about language

LAP teachers reported that explicit teaching helps children better understand language concepts. They found that children were fascinated by language. They wanted to know about their own language and the languages of their friends. They were especially intrigued by the language backgrounds and abilities of their teachers. They shared the names of familiar objects in their home languages, attempted to pronounce words in each other's languages and identified with their language groups. They also came to understand that people 'have' and 'speak' languages.

The two examples that follow are from a kindergarten classroom where the teacher talked to the children about language, shared books about language with them, and directly taught them language concepts. Here are two things I witnessed in this classroom.

'You, how you talk at home?'

As I entered the kindergarten classroom, Bahadur came up to me and asked, 'You, how you talk at home?' I told him that I speak Ukrainian. My new friend looked puzzled, directed me to a globe and said: 'Show me.' I responded by pointing to Ukraine and explained that 'my language' is also spoken by many people in Canada. I showed him the Cyrillic alphabet and made a Ukrainian name card for him (see below). By this time, four other children had joined us. We talked about writing systems, translations and the difference between

Bahadur	Багадур

Figure 4.2 Navid's green book

'knowing' and 'using' a language. When it was time for me to leave, I said 'Бувай здоровий!' ('Keep well') to my new friend. He turned to his classmate and proudly said: 'That's how she says "bye"'.

'Here's my book. It's in my language. Wanna see?'

One day, Navid, a Farsi-English bilingual, arrived in his Kindergarten classroom with a thin green book under his arm (Figure 4.2). He approached me, held the book up high and announced: 'Here's my book. It's in my language. Wanna see? I'll show you but it's my book.' Turning to a classmate who was standing close by, Navid continued: 'It's my book. And I can show you. You can see too.' Throughout the morning Navid shared his book with his classmates. Their response is noteworthy: they looked at the Farsi text with awe and great interest. Navid repeated the same words ('It's my book. And I can show you. You can see too.') Beaming with pride, he watched his friends examine the book. Picking up on this interest, the teacher invited Navid's mother to come to the class to explain the Farsi language to the children.

Challenge 3: Single speakers of home languages

Some LAP classrooms include children who are single speakers of 'little known' languages. Here are three examples: Twi (spoken in Ghana), Kutchi (spoken in India and Pakistan) and Wú (spoken in Shanghai and Hong Kong). LAP teachers reported that speakers of these languages were unwilling to talk about their home languages and that their classmates find the names of their language 'silly' and 'stupid'.

In the following example, a Grade 2 teacher brought the children together to talk about Kutchi, the home language of Aarusha. Using a map and a globe, this is how she proceeded:

'Aarusha speaks a language called Kutchi. She is the only one in our class who speaks this language. Let's ask her to help us understand the Kutchi language. I wonder if there are other children in our school who speak Kutchi. Let's ask the principal.'

'Kutchi is a language with more than 11 million speakers worldwide. This means that many people speak Kutchi.'

Using a map, the teacher asks Aarusha to help her mark the countries where Kutchi is spoken.

'Most Kutchi speakers live in India in the Kutch region of Gujarat, and also in Sindh in Pakistan. There are also some Kutchi speakers in Africa, England and the United States. There are Kutchi speakers in Canada. We have a Kutchi speaker, Aarusha, in our class.'

'This is the way we write Kutchi in English. And this pink chart shows Kutchi writing. Kutchi is also known as Cutchi, Kutchhi or Kachchhi. Dog in Kutchi is "kutoo", cat is "bilaadee".'

Let's invite Aarusha's mom or dad to come to our class and tell us more about the Kutchi language."

Challenge 4: Partnering with families

LAP teachers understand the importance of partnering with families. They know that when teachers and parents work together to support and encourage learning, children achieve more, feel confident, love school and want to learn. Yet LAP teachers report that partnering with families is not always easy. Some parents say that they are too busy to participate in their child's school life. Others feel uncertain and uncomfort-  able in the classroom. Also, connecting with newcomer families can be challenging. While some are unfamiliar with the idea of parental school engagement, others avoid participation due to their limited command of the school language. All of this leaves LAP teachers wondering how best to connect with families.

Develop partnerships with families

In order to develop meaningful partnerships with families, LAP teachers take two actions: they gather information and put partnering strategies in place. Let's have a closer look at these two actions.

Gather information: Know your families

According to home-school researchers (Jiang, 2011; López, 2001; Moll, 1992), partnerships with families will be meaningful only when teachers have an accurate understanding of countries, cultures, religious practices, world languages and literacies, various forms of parental engagement, children's home experiences and family 'funds of knowledge'.

Use a short questionnaire (see sample below) to collect information about children's families and backgrounds.

Sample questionnaire

Dear parents and families,
    Please answer the questions below and return this Questionnaire to the school.

(1) Child's name _____

(2) Child's country of birth _____

(3) Father's country of birth _____

(4) Mother's country of birth _____

(5) Do grandparents live with you? _____

(6) Language or languages spoken in the home: _____

(7) Do you share books with your child? In which language? How often? _____
_____

(8) Religion _____

(9) Special celebrations in your family _____

(10) List your family's talents, hobbies and skills. For example: music, arts, sports, crafts. _____

Thank you.

The responses from the questionnaires will provide you with basic information about each family. Your next task is to extend this information and create profiles of each country of origin represented in your class. These profiles will include geographic, linguistic, cultural and religious facts. An example follows.

A profile of Somalia

Looking over the questionnaire responses, Paul (a Grade 3 teacher) discovered that the children in his class (and their families) came from the following countries: Canada, the USA, Somalia, Russia, Pakistan, Hong Kong, Thailand, Sri Lanka and China. To extend his understanding of these countries, Paul consulted the internet and prepared 'fact' profiles for each country. Completed profiles were shared and exchanged with colleagues and stored on his computer.

To prepare the following one-page Somalia fact profile, Paul consulted two sources:

• YouTube clip: Somalis; Origins, History, & Culture
• YouTube clip: Somali Culture Day 12/2015 (https://www.youtube.com/watch?v=xshIS1KzvHs)

Somalia

- located in eastern, mainland Africa
- situated on the peninsula known as the Horn of Africa
- created in 1960 from a former British protectorate and an Italian colony
- currently without a central government since President was overthrown in 1991
- much of the territory has been subject to serious civil strife
- capital city: Mogadishu
- population 10.8 million (UN: 2015)
- major languages Somali, Arabic, Italian and English
- 99.8% of Somalia's population is Muslim: the majority belong to the Sunni branch of Islam
- currency: Somali shilling
- Somalia is a semi-arid country with about 1.64% arable land
- hot conditions year-round, along with periodic monsoon winds and irregular rainfall
- mean daily maximum temperatures range from 30 to 40°C (86 to 104°F)
- Somalia contains a variety of mammals due to its geographical and climatic diversity
- wild fauna are found throughout the territory, including the cheetah, lion, baboon and elephant
- currently home to around 727 species of birds
- has the largest population of camels in the world
- the camel provides transportation, milk, meat and income
- Somali and Arabic are the official languages of Somalia
- Somali language is the mother tongue of the Somali people, the nation's most populous ethnic group
- English is widely spoken and taught
- Somali has been written with a number of different scripts, including Arabic-based
- the Latin alphabet was adopted in 1972 and Somali was made the sole official language of Somalia
- Qu'ranic schools remain the basic system of traditional religious instruction in Somalia
- all food is served halal (an Arabic word that means 'permissible')
- soccer is the most popular sport in Somalia
- henna is an important part of Somali culture and is worn by women on hands, arms, feet and neck during weddings, Eid and Ramadan
- most Somali women wear full-length dresses that come in a variety of styles

Partnering strategies

With your new understanding of children's backgrounds, you are now ready to partner with families.

Here are five partnering strategies:

- Sharing information with newcomer families
- Inviting families to share their skills and talents
- Welcoming grandparents
- Creating family stories
- Staying connected

Strategy 1: Sharing information with newcomer families

LAP teachers are encouraged to share information about childhood bilingualism with newcomer families. This will help dispel the misconceptions that many parents have about children's dual-language learning, such as the widespread (and erroneous) belief that bilingual children are confused. This will also provide families with updated, accurate and research-based information about children's dual-language learning and encourage them to maintain their home languages. Here are three resources to share with families: a bilingual myth-fact table, a brochure and a resource list.

Bilingual myths – and facts

In Table 4.2, bilingual myths and facts are presented side-by-side in an easy-to-read format. This table can be posted on the classroom website (or blog) or you can send hard copies home. Another way to share the information is to organize a 'bilingual' evening for families and present the information, leaving time for questions and discussion.

Table 4.2 Bilingual myths and facts

Bilingual myths: Not true!	Bilingual facts: True!
Young children acquire a second language with ease and require no support.	Young children require a language-rich environment and meaningful interaction to acquire a second language.
Learning two languages is confusing to children.	Learning two languages is *not* confusing to young children.
Using the home language will hinder progress in the classroom language.	Using the home language will help the child make progress in the school language.
Young children can only manage one language at time.	With sufficient exposure, support and guidance, young children can manage two languages at the same time.
A child who learns two languages will never be comfortable in either of them.	A child who learns two languages will be enriched by two cultures.
The two languages of a bilingual work separately and should be separated.	The two languages of a bilingual work together and influence one another.

If you want your children to succeed then HOLD ON to your home language!

This short, eight-page, brightly coloured brochure is prepared especially for parents. It is available in 21 languages, (Arabic, Chinese, Dutch, English, Farsi, Filipino, French, Gujarati, Hungarian, Icelandic, Italian, Japanese, Korean, Polish, Punjabi, Romanian, Russian, Spanish, Ukrainian, Urdu and Turkish) and provides the following information in an easy-to-read format:

- home languages are important;
- reasons for maintaining the home language;
- the advantages for children who use two languages;
- how two languages work together;
- speaking the home language will *not* confuse children;
- a foundation in the home language helps children learn the school language; and
- suggestions for maintaining the home language.

The HOLD ON brochure can be downloaded free of charge from https://www.ryerson.ca/mylanguage/brochures/.

Resources for families

In Chapter 5 you will find resources to share with families. Post them on your classroom blog or make a list and send it home. LAP teachers will also find important information in these resources.

Strategy 2: Inviting families to share their skills and talents

Invite families to share their skills, talents and languages. Two sample letters are provided to help you get started. Prepare a 'sharing' schedule and align the invitations with your ongoing curriculum.

Strategy 3: Welcome grandparents

Grandparents are special people for many children. They are also an invaluable classroom multilingual resource. Unlike busy working parents, grandparents have time to come to the classroom to share their 'funds of knowledge'. In Chapter 5 you will find a list of picture books about grandparents to share with young children. Strategies for involving grandparents in the classroom can be found in LAP12 (pp. 124–126).

Strategy 4: Creating family stories

Bringing families together to create personal storybooks is a tried-and-true partnering strategy (Ada & Campoy, 2003; Bernhard *et al*., 2008). In this multilingual initiative, families meet to chat, share their stories and create books. Children are

Sample letter: Invitation to families to share their skills and talents

Dear mom, dad and family,

Thank you for completing the questionnaire.

Our families are talented and gifted. Here is a list of reported skills, talents and hobbies:

soccer coach, dentist, baker, piano teacher, henna artist, yoga teacher, computer programmer, dog walker, guitar player, seven-string zither player, hand drum player, stamp collector and hockey player

You are invited to come to our class to share your skills and talents with us. Our skills and talents sharing day is Wednesday, from 1:00 to 2:00 pm.

The skills and talents sharing schedule is posted inside the classroom door. Sign up and share what you know and love with us!

We look forward to seeing you in our classroom.

Sample letter: Invitation to families to share their languages

Dear mom, dad and family,

Thank you for completing the questionnaire.

Our multilingual classroom

The children in our classroom speak many different languages. At last count, we had speakers of 10 languages: Mandarin, Polish, Hebrew, English, Urdu, Tamil, Tagalog, Portuguese, Yoruba and German.

Our teachers are also speakers of a number of languages. In addition to English, Miss Pearl speaks Mandarin, Miss Luiska speaks Polish and Mr Tahir is a speaker of Urdu. Our classroom door is open to all languages. Knowing how important languages are, we support and promote bilingualism.

Share your languages!

Throughout the year, we will help all children learn and grow in English. We will also support families who are speakers of the many languages listed above. In our lessons and activities, we will include home languages. We will talk about different ways of speaking, writing and reading.

We invite you to come and share your languages with us. Our language sharing day is Friday, from 1:00 to 2:00 pm. The language-sharing schedule is posted inside the classroom door. Sign up and share your language with us.

We look forward to seeing you in our classroom.

encouraged to participate and select experiences to write about. Dual-language texts are prepared and visuals such as photographs and drawings are added. Technological devices (computers, tablets, cameras, cell phones) are used to translate text, add audio-clips and plan layout. Completed books are printed, laminated, bound and shared. Copies are displayed in the school library, are added to the classroom library and are also sent home.

The family story initiative is far from a one-time happening. Families and children are encouraged to create additional books at home, share them with classmates and add them to the classroom book collection.

Strategy 5: Staying connected
Allison Kennedy

In order to keep families connected and updated, many LAP teachers create and maintain a classroom blog. This includes information about classroom, school and community events. Links to community websites will connect families to events and happenings. A translation feature (Figure 4.3) will help newcomer families.

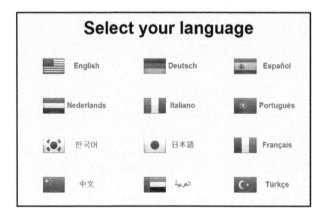

Figure 4.3 Sample translation feature

Sample blog message

Hello everyone,

Thank you for visiting our website.

Visit us often for updates on classroom happenings and projects, links to valuable resources, and activities to do with your child at home.

Consider this …

(1) What challenges have you encountered in your multilingual teaching?
(2) How do you talk to young children about language?
(3) Visit the public library with your class. Ask the librarian to explain the multi-lingual collection.
(4) What are the benefits of explicit teaching?
(5) Organize a 'Bilingual' workshop for families. Use the 'Bilingual-Myth/Bilingual-Fact' chart and the 'Hold On' brochure to engage participants in a discussion about children's dual-language development and home language maintenance.

References

Ada, A.F. and Campoy, I. (2003) *Authors in the Classroom: A Transformative Education Process.* New York: Pearson.

Bernhard, J.K., Winsler, A., Bleiker, C., Ginieniewicz, J. and Madigan, A. (2008) Read my story: Promoting early literacy among diverse, urban, preschool children in poverty with the Early Authors Program. *Journal of Education for Students Placed at Risk* 13 (1), 76–105.

Jiang, F. (2011) Chinese immigrant parents' communication with their children's school teachers: Experiences, expectations and challenges. *Electronic Theses and Dissertations* 247. See https://scholar.uwindsor.ca/cgi/viewcontent.cgi?article=1246&context=etd.

López, G.R. (2001) The value of hard work: Lessons on parent involvement from an (im)migrant household. *Harvard Educational Review* 71, 416–437.

Moll, L.C., Amanti, C., Neff, D. and González, N. (1992) Funds of knowledge for teaching: Using a qualitative approach to connect homes and classrooms. *Theory into Practice* 31 (2), 132–141.

5 LAP Resources

The resources in this chapter will help you move your LAP agenda forward. The first resource is a six-point LAP guide. This professional tool will help you identify, position and plan your multilingual work. Following this you will find book lists, websites, suggestions and ideas to enrich and extend your multilingual teaching. Here is a list of the multilingual resources as they appear in the chapter. The names of contributors are included with each resource.

(1) LAP Guide
(2) Professional Reading
(3) Children's Books
(4) Books and Websites to Share with Families
(5) Singing and Language Learning
(6) A Resource from Germany
(7) A Resource from Sweden
(8) Indigenous Languages
(9) International Mother Language Day
(10) Scribjab
(11) Home Language Story Sharing
(12) Connecting Newcomers
(13) Living Together: Muslims in a Changing World
(14) Homework for Newcomers
(15) Five more LAP activities

Resource 1: The LAP Guide

The LAP guide (Figure 5.1) consists of six building blocks. Each block represents a progressive step towards the understanding and the adoption of multilingual teaching.

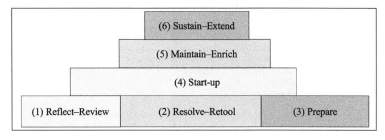

Figure 5.1 The six building blocks of the LAP guide

As you review the guide, identify the position that best matches your current multilingual work.

Using the LAP guide

As you review the LAP guide, think about a best-selling book entitled *Never Eat Alone*. In it, the author, Keith Ferrazzi (2014), makes a strong case for connecting and working together. When people connect and share, he writes, everyone grows and wins. The same principle applies here. Review the LAP guide with colleagues who teach the same grade or level. Working together and exchanging ideas about multilingual teaching will allow you to learn together, support each other and improve your multilingual agenda.

Building block 1: Reflect–Review

In Building block 1, teachers become aware of the diversity in their classrooms. They witness the growing number of children who do not speak the school language and begin to wonder what this means for their teaching. As they reach out to newcomers, they realize that their tried-and-true monolingual strategies do not seem to work.

When faced with this situation, teachers engage in personal and professional reflection and review. On the personal level, they think about their own language experiences such as languages they speak, languages they once tried to learn, and perhaps languages they forgot or lost. On the professional level, teachers in the Reflect–Review position think about bilingualism and review their instructional practice. They then think about practice change.

Building block 2: Resolve–Retool

In Building block 2, teachers refer to Table 5.1 to identify their current practice with newcomers. They realize, for example, that assimilative and supportive practice does not work in linguistically diverse classrooms. They turn their attention to inclusive or multilingual practice and decide to change direction in their teaching.

Table 5.1 Instructional practices with newcomers

Practice	Goals	Focus	Sample strategies
Assimilative	• Help children learn the school language. • Absorb them into the majority language and culture.	• School language and literacy.	• Separate children who speak the same language. • Encourage parents to speak the school language at home.
Supportive	• Help children learn the school language. • Acknowledge home languages and cultures.	• School language and literacy. • Acknowledgment of home languages and cultures.	• Learn key words in children's home languages. • Acknowledge home languages. • Organize multicultural activities.
Inclusive LAP	• Help children learn the school language. • Promote home languages and multilingualism. • Bring home languages and literacies into the classroom.	• School language and literacy. • Home languages and literacies.	• Read, share and create dual-language books. • Announce news in the school language and also in home languages. • Invite families to share languages and literacies.

Building block 3: Prepare

Having made the decision to retool their instructional practice, teachers in Building block 3 set out to understand the *what*, *why* and *how* of multilingual teaching. They consult guidebooks, attend multilingual workshops and connect with colleagues who are familiar with LAP.

Building block 4: Start-up

Teachers in Building block 4 take their first LAP steps. They document children's language backgrounds, create language and family profiles and start making home languages seen and heard in their classrooms.

Building block 5: Maintain–Enrich

Teachers in the Maintain–Enrich block are committed to LAP. Their classrooms are multilingual environments where home languages are seen, heard, used and included in the curriculum. They encourage children to use their home languages in the classroom, provide language choice for classroom projects and interaction, pair children who speak the same languages, make extensive use of multilingual resources and welcome families to share their languages, literacies and knowledge.

Building block 6: Sustain–Extend

In these classrooms, children use the language or languages that work best for them. The curriculum has a home language component, and literacy is encouraged and supported both in the school language and in home languages. As teachers guide learning from the local to the global, initiatives and projects extend beyond the classroom to include families and the wider school community. Teachers in the Sustain–Extend block are multilingual advocates and activists. They welcome new multilingual challenges, collaborate with colleagues, mentor those who are new to LAP, participate in multilingual workshops and conferences and develop multilingual resources.

Resource 2: Professional Reading

Reading list

There are hundreds, if not thousands, of publications about multilingualism and multilingual teaching. The sheer number of books, journal articles and brochures can be overwhelming, leaving LAP teachers wondering which ones will best inform their teaching. To get you started, a list of basic readings is provided in the Appendix.

Professional Book Club

Organize a professional book club with colleagues who teach the same grade or level, or with your entire school staff. Read and discuss the readings provided in the Appendix. Communal reading is important for a number of reasons:

- It helps you gain insight into your own strengths and talents. For example, are you a leader, an ideas person, an organizer, an innovator, a team builder or a change-maker?
- It brings about personal, curricular and organizational change.
- It helps to build better working relationships among colleagues, including mentorship relationships between experienced and new teachers.
- It creates a forum for exploring new teaching ideas or addressing perceived (or unperceived) problems and concerns.
- It helps teachers make a connection between theory and practice through the sharing of 'real world' classroom experiences inspired by the readings.
- It gives all colleagues a voice.

The following website provides tips and suggestions for organizing a professional book club: https://www.scribd.com/document/132710748/Tips-for-Your-Professional-Development-Book-Club (accessed 2 February 2018).

Getting started

Decide on a name for your professional book club. Start your book club by viewing this short YouTube clip which provides the highlights of LAP: https://www.youtube.com/watch?v=wLod5d9mT98 (accessed 30 January 2018).

Resource 3: Children's Books

Book lists

In the Appendix you will find these book lists:

- picture books about refugee children and newcomers;
- books for children about language; and
- books about grandparents.

Multilingual children's library collections

Most public and school libraries in linguistically diverse neighbourhoods have multilingual children's collections. These collections are sorted alphabetically by language and include dual-language books. Here are some tips to help you take full advantage of these collections.

- Visit the public library and connect with the librarian.
- Check out the multilingual children's collection. Which languages are included in the collection?
- Schedule regular visits to the public library with your class.
- Ask the librarian to give your class a tour of the library and explain the multilingual collection.
- Encourage the children to find and read books in their home languages.
- Plan topic-specific visits that align with your curriculum.
- Invite the librarian to visit your classroom.

Multilingual children's digital book collections

Children's multilingual books can also be found on the internet. In the Appendix you will find 10 websites of video- and audio-clips, dual-language books for sale and also free-access books.

Storybooks Canada, Indigenous Storybooks and Global Storybooks

Bonny Norton

To help children learn English (or French) as well as maintain the home language, a University of British Columbia team under the leadership of Bonny Norton, a professor in the Department of Language and Literacy Education, developed Storybooks Canada (www.storybookscanada.ca). This website has been designed specifically for teachers, parents and community members, making 40 stories from the African Storybook (www.africanstorybook.org) freely available in the major immigrant and refugee languages of Canada, as well as in English and French. The team has also developed a sister site in Canada called Indigenous Storybooks (http://indigenousstorybooks. ca/), led by Sara Davidson of the University of the Fraser Valley.

What is unique about Storybooks Canada?

This website not only offers beautifully illustrated children's stories in many languages, but it interlinks these stories so that the user can easily switch between English and one of the other available languages. In this way, a class can read a story in English, and individual students can check the translation of the story in their home language, page by page. Storybooks Canada also provides audio-recordings, a feature that allows users to listen to the story even if they can't read the text in their own language.

The Glitterlings[1]

Eithne Gallagher

The Glitterlings is a delightful series which includes nine storybooks, an accompanying CD and a Teacher's Resource Book. Described as 'interlingual' and 'play-based' by the author, Eithne Gallagher, the Glitterlings are four brightly coloured bouncy creatures that live on a planet that is 'two stars left of the moon'. Glitterlings are polyglots who love languages and enjoy listening to all the different languages coming from planet Earth. The Glitterlings travel from their planet to Ms Glyn's classroom, a place '… full of fun and discovery, languages and songs', where they learn and share languages (for example, Panda language), meet new friends and witness experiences (e.g. transition from home to classroom, joining a new language environment, understanding language similarities and differences, friendship and sharing) that are both relevant and meaningful to newcomers. In a playful and lively manner, the Glitterlings stories remind children that languages can be shared, discovered and explored, that they matter, that they are fun, that they should be valued and respected and that they are an important part of one's identity. For suggestions on using The Glitterlings books with children, go to the Appendix.

The Best of All Worlds – Le meilleur monde imaginable
One book – seven stories – nine languages

Serena Quintal and Gina Valle

'This book will enable children to develop a heightened awareness of different cultures and promote a respect for diversity'

Canadian Commission for UNESCO

This multilingual collection was published in partnership with the Canadian Commission for UNESCO as an International Mother Language Day project. According to Gina Valle, the Canadian-Italian editor, its purpose is to 'honour home languages and cultures' and help children understand and respect diversity. The seven original stories, presented in nine languages (Arabic, English, Farsi, French, Italian, Japanese, Portuguese, Russian and Spanish) are intended as a resource for teachers working in linguistically diverse classrooms (Grades 1–6). The Teachers' Resource that accompanies the book links the stories to the various subject strand expectations of the Ontario Curriculum. Both book and Teachers' Resource are available from www. AtOnePress.ca. Suggestions for using this multilingual book can be found in the Appendix.

The Dual Language Showcase

The Dual Language Showcase was launched in 1998. It is an ongoing collection of dual-language books created by children from a highly diverse school near Toronto. Hard copies of the books are included in the school library. For more information about the Dual-Language Showcase, visit http://schools.peelschools.org/1363/DualLanguage/Documents/index.htm.

Dual-language book reading: A resource for teachers and teacher educators

Rahat Zaidi

This series of lesson plans was prepared by Rahat Zaidi from the University of Calgary. It includes strategies for sharing dual-language books in English-medium classrooms. The resource includes 10 dual-language books. In addition to English, the stories appear in Spanish, Urdu, French and Tagalog. The books are published by Mantra Lingua and are available at http://uk.mantralingua.com/.

For a demonstration of how these books have been used in Canada, go to http://www.rahatnaqvi.ca/wordpress/dual-language-books-project/ (accessed 30 April 2018).

See also Zaidi, R. (2018) *A Proposal for 21st Century Education: An Introduction to Dual Language Book Reading.* Konect Teaching Materials, Vol. 6. Barcelona: Konect Project. See https://docs.wixstatic.com/ugd/d3edd2_c9a71a9fa1c3434096693f841d676326.pdf.

Resource 4: Books and Websites to Share with Families

Books and websites about bilingualism intended for families are listed in the Appendix.

Your Home Language: Foundation for Success

This 12-minute DVD provides suggestions for home language activities that parents, family members and caregivers can enjoy together with children to encourage language development and success at school. It is available in English, Bengali, Punjabi, Russian, Somali, Farsi, Spanish, Gujarati, Tamil, Korean, Urdu, Mandarin and Vietnamese. See https://vimeo.com/21752842.

Resource 5: Singing and Language Learning

Bobby Abrol, Jenni Alisaari, Leena Maria Heikkola and Charlene Ryan

LAP teachers know that children with little or no command of the school language respond enthusiastically and positively to singing. These educators report that singing touches these children in powerful and important ways: it eases their integration into the classroom, naturally engages them and helps them connect with classmates and make friends. LAP teachers also know that guarded, hesitant newcomers often 'awaken' to singing.

In this report, four educators share their views on the importance and power of singing.

- Charlene, a Canadian music teacher and researcher, explains the role singing plays in our lives generally and the importance of singing for children's development and learning.
- Jenni and Leena, two music researchers and former language teachers from Finland, describe how singing enhances newcomers' language learning.
- Bobby, a classroom teacher working in India, describes how she brought singing into her linguistically diverse classroom.

Charlene: The importance of singing

Singing is a pervasive and powerful human behaviour. It features prominently in religious, family and community celebrations across a vast array of cultures. Singing can provoke intense memories, responses and emotions in adults and children alike. Babies are calmed through singing (even in unfamiliar languages), more effectively than through the spoken word (Corbeil *et al.*, 2016). Perhaps this is why infant-directed speech, our early communication with babies, bears much similarity to song (Malloch & Trevarthen, 2008).

> 'Jump in and share the joy of song...!'
>
> '... put aside your fears and self-consciousness and bring the extraordinary tool of song to your multilingual work. You do not need to be a rock star (or operatic one, either) to sing with children. You simply need to be willing to jump in and share the joy of song with them.'

Research on singing increasingly shows its potential benefits to brain activation, overall health and the basic human experience. It has been associated with the release of endorphins, which likely contributes to the positive experience we have while singing (Dunbar *et al.*, 2012). For children, music – and in particular singing – is associated with play and is believed to contribute to social development (Ilari, 2016). Indeed, the importance of music and the tremendous value that children place on song makes them particularly potent vehicles through which extra-musical skills, such as language acquisition, may be achieved (Campbell, 2010).

Languages are complex. Learning a new language is challenging, with effective communication requiring the mastery of many components that may be tedious to learn. The overlap between speech and song, in terms of the production of sound and the implicated brain regions, is certainly a valid reason to include song in language learning. More than this, though, the addition of music to speech brings joy and meaning to the experience. Can you imagine learning the letters of the alphabet without a tune in mind? The repetition of 26 letters through speech would seem tiresome to the most patient of learners. Yet, through the miracle of song, young children happily sing the alphabet repeatedly and frequently, with pride and enthusiasm.

Indeed, many classroom teachers use song to encourage the memorization of all sorts of rote material. The engagement that music typically brings motivates children to practise often and gleefully, becoming increasingly fluent in the material. Basic lists such as the alphabet, the days of the week and the months of the year, as well as pre-school and primary class routines, are all learned and repeated over and over in the form of song. My own four-year-old daughter will happily sing the 'months-of-the-year' song for all who will listen. Yet, if she were asked to memorize this same material as a simple spoken list, I doubt the inclination to practise and refine would remain. In even the simplest of songs, melody and rhythm come together in such a powerful and infectious way that their impact on learning cannot be underestimated.

Jenni and Leena: Singing and language learning go hand-in-hand

Some background

Songs and poems have been used in language teaching for many years. In the United States, for example, guidelines for using singing in language classrooms were published as early as the 1980s (James, 1985). In recent years there have been a growing number of studies reporting that music and singing enhance language learning (Abbott, 2002; Alisaari, 2015; Legg, 2009). Other positive effects of music, like an increased sense of togetherness, have also been documented (Wiltermuth & Heath, 2009).

What research tells us about the benefits of singing

Research tells us that singing is good for children and that it is particularly beneficial for language learners.

Social benefits of singing

Singing in the classroom has been linked to positive group dynamics (Lake, 2003). It has been found to increase learners' sense of togetherness and helpfulness towards each other (Spychiger *et al.*, 1995; Wiltermuth & Heath, 2009). Singing also offers a good opportunity to interact with others when language skills are still limited, allowing children to participate (Domoney & Harris, 1993).

> 'Do you sing with children?
>
> If so, have you noticed how quickly the atmosphere becomes joyful? Why is it that language learners learn song lyrics so easily?'

Personal benefits of singing

Children can enjoy singing even if they do not understand everything they hear. First, they can hum along to a song or just listen (Lems, 2005). They can then sing the refrain and gradually sing other parts (Lake, 2003). Singing creates a relaxed and enjoyable atmosphere in the language-learning classroom and reduces anxiety in novice language learners. This is important, since language learning is most effective when learners feel safe, are in 'low anxiety' and have a positive attitude towards learning (Krashen, 2009). If music helps to make the learning environment safe, children are more likely to feel confident and take risks in learning situations (Hakkarainen *et al.*, 2005).

Language-learning benefits of singing

Singing offers newcomers the following benefits:

- learn in enjoyable ways;
- learn without understanding everything;
- learn words, structures and phrases, pronunciation and speech patterns;
- practise the new language involuntarily with 'stuck-in-my-head' songs;
- improve oral fluency; and
- engage in rhythmic movement (stomp, clap and dance) to remember.

Jenni and Leena study singing with language learners

In one study, we investigated the effect of singing on the learning of Finnish grammar. The participants in our study were 10 newcomers (10–12 years old) who were starting to learn Finnish. After a four-week period of singing we noted the following:

- song lyrics helped the children learn grammatical structures;
- children started producing grammatical structures that were previously only understood; and
- singing helped hesitant, silent children open up and start using Finnish.

Bobby: Singing to the rescue!

Faced with 60 Grade 3 children who spoke 16 different languages, Bobby wondered about experiences that could be shared with the entire class. She asked herself: 'What can work as a starting point for sharing?' The answer came as she watched children enter the classroom singing songs they had learned at home.

Picking up on this, Bobby launched the 'Singer of the Day' project. This initiative started with songs in the children's home languages and included drawing, reading and writing. Using various cultural symbols, children illustrated their interpretation of songs. A spontaneous and natural next step was the 'Magic Sentence for Today', where song lyrics were written out both in the school and home languages and labels and narratives were created for the drawings.

Bobby calls this project a 'pedagogical discovery'. It surprised her because, in her words: 'I didn't know anything about music, other than I enjoy it.' She refers to the literacy component of the project as 'golden learning moments' that had personal meaning for the children.

Read more about Bobby's project here: Abrol, B. (2014) Drawing songs of literacy in a multilingual classroom. *TESOL Connections*, July. See http://newsmanager.com-mpartners.com/tesolc/downloads/features/2014/2014-07_Songs.pdf.

Tips for singing in the LAP classroom

As the above reports show, singing and language learning go together. The suggestions found here come from music educators and the author's field notes. As you read them, think about how you can add or extend singing to your multilingual agenda.

Keep it short, simple and fun

Choose your songs carefully. Length, rhythm, melody, tempo, theme, pronunciation and age appropriateness should all be taken into account (Kilgour *et al.*, 2000). The melody and rhythm of the song should be moderately simple. Also, songs with clear pronunciation are important for children learning a new language.

Point, jump and repeat

Choose interactive songs. Gestures, actions and repetition make singing enjoyable and memorable. Gestures and actions help newcomers understand and remember lyrics and learn new words and phrases. For example, if the word 'stomach' is in the lyrics, encourage children to point to their stomachs. Repeated phrases can be reinforced beyond the singing experience and be included in literacy activities.

Translate popular songs into home languages

With the help of older children, families and colleagues, translate popular songs into home languages. Figure 5.2 shows the Urdu translation of 'Hickory-Dickory-Dock'.

A multilingual version: 'How far I'll go'

'How far I'll go' is a song from the children's movie 'Moana'. In this video-clip it is sung in 24 languages: https://www.youtube.com/watch?v = 0g29Wg4oyek (accessed 4 April 2018).

Share this video-clip with your class and, working together, create a list of the 24 languages. Ask children whose languages are not included to provide translations.

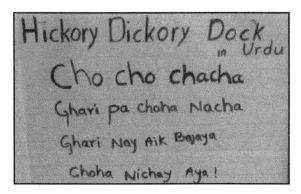

Figure 5.2 Hickory-Dickory-Dock in Urdu

Resource 6: From Germany

Zentrum für Mehrsprachigkeit und Integration: ZMI, Köln [Centre for Multilingualism and Integration, Cologne]

> 'Newly arrived migrant students in German schools are currently the centre of attention.'
>
> Terhart and von Dewits (2018)

The Center for Multilingualism and Integration[2] is a partnership institution between the District Government of Cologne, the city of Cologne and the University of Cologne (Germany). Created in 2008, the goal of the ZMI is to promote the German language and 'establish, continue and expand joint activities on multilingualism and integration' at all educational levels and across languages.

The ZMI:

- initiates and supports projects in multilingualism and integration in elementary education, adult education and teacher training and research; and
- supports educational institutions in their efforts to systematically and permanently implement the promotion of German and multilingual education, thus contributing to the intercultural opening up of the Cologne educational landscape.

Resource 7: From Sweden

Flerspråkighet: Alla barn, alla språk, alla dagar! [Multilingualism: All children, all languages, every day!]

This resource, which has been called the 'Swedish LAP', is for kindergarten and primary level teachers working in linguistically diverse classrooms in Sweden.

The author, Mahroo Khousravi, is a Farsi-Swedish bilingual who was born in Iran and lives in Sweden. She teaches in a linguistically diverse preschool in Mölndal where, in addition to Swedish and sign language, the children speak over 30 different languages. In addition to her teaching, Mahroo is involved in the preparation of multilingual resources for teachers. Her book includes a discussion of the importance and benefits of bilingualism and provides suggestions for integrating multilingualism into the prescribed curriculum. Anneli, a Swedish as a second language teacher, describes the book as 'inspirational and helpful'.

Resource 8: Exploring Indigenous Languages with Children

In response to the endangerment, loss and disappearance of Indigenous languages worldwide, the United Nations General Assembly adopted a Resolution on 'Rights of Indigenous Peoples', proclaiming 2019 as the International Year of Indigenous Languages. The Action plan for this special year calls on 'a range of stakeholders' to do their part, 'participate actively' and organize events, projects and initiatives to promote and protect Indigenous languages. See http://www.un.org/en/ga/search/view_doc.asp?symbol = E/C.19/2018/8.

 Ways in which LAP teachers can respond to the International Year of Indigenous Languages call for action

(1) Familiarize yourself with the Indigenous populations and languages of your country.
(2) In an age-appropriate way, engage children in discussion about Indigenous people and their languages.
(3) Invite children to research and document Indigenous languages, learn basic words, create multilingual displays and share information.
(4) Connect with an Indigenous family or group. Invite speakers to visit your classroom to share their languages.
(5) Plan a school-wide Indigenous event to celebrate the Indigenous languages of your country.

Resource 9: International Mother Language Day

In 1999 the United Nations Educational, Scientific and Cultural Organization (UNESCO) proclaimed 21 February as International Mother Language Day (IMLD). The purpose of this day is 'to promote the preservation and protection of all languages used by peoples of the world' and 'to promote unity in diversity and international understanding, through multilingualism and multiculturalism'.

IMLD activities

(1) Visit the UNESCO website for IMLD resources; see http://www.un.org/en/events/ motherlanguageday/ (accessed 8 January 2018).
(2) Invite children to create their own IMLD posters and display them in class.
(3) List the languages included in this video-clip: https://www.youtube.com/ watch?v=aMDxUFbkE_M.
(4) Plan an IMLD school or classroom concert. Invite the children to plan the programme, invite families and community members, send out invitations and video-record the event.
(5) Create a school language map listing all the languages spoken by the school community.

Resource 10: Scribjab

Kelleen Toohey

Scribjab is a website and iPad application developed by Kelleen Toohey from Simon Fraser University. It was built on the premise that children learn second languages faster and better if they have a strong foundation in their first language. ScribJab invites children to read, create and share digital stories in English, French or their home language. Space is provided for young readers and authors to discuss their stories with one another. Teachers can monitor and organize children's contributions and create reading groups.

For a tour of Scribjab go to http://scribjab.com/en/about/tour.html.

Resource 11: Home Language Story Sharing

Marina Petrovic and Suzanne Muir

The idea of sharing stories in home languages during the school lunch hour was put forward by author, teacher and librarian Suzanne Muir. Working in a linguistically diverse elementary school in southern Ontario, Suzanne collaborated with English-language teachers, teachers who were speakers of the children's home languages and families to 'build community' and bring the children's home languages into the school. The home language story time is held in the school library, lasts approximately 20 minutes and is intended for children in Grades 1–3.

During story sessions, mostly dual-language picture books are shared with the children. In some cases teachers and parents shared information books that were directly related to ongoing curriculum topics. Between 20 and 30 children attend the book-sharing sessions. Even though the children do not understand all of the languages in which books are read, they listen and appear interested in the languages of others.

Response to the home language story sharing is positive on all fronts. The children are excited to listen to stories in their home languages and also to the languages of their friends. Parents are happy that their languages are included in the school agenda. Interest spread to other schools, who expressed an interest in organizing home language book sharing.

Resource 12: Connecting Newcomers

Tracy Wheatley-Romano

The Halton District School Board[3] has a highly diverse student population and continues to accept newcomer students. Of the 60 different languages spoken by Halton students, Urdu, Mandarin, Arabic, Punjabi and Hindi are the most numerous.

The purpose of the board-wide Innovative Initiative is to help newcomers transition into their new classrooms and schools. Following the initial 'welcome' process, newcomers, teachers and student ambassadors (former newcomers and speakers of many languages) connect virtually (via Google Hangout)[4] to provide basic information and arrange a meeting. When the newcomers arrive in their new school they are welcomed by the teachers and the student ambassadors they have met on Google Hangout. Using the newcomer's language, the student ambassadors help them navigate their new school. Teachers report that the Innovative Initiative gives newcomers a voice, eases their transition to their new school, and helps them make friends and integrate into the life of the classroom.

For more information about the Halton Innovative Project, see https://www.youtube.com/watch?v=XY9YtbkWWys (accessed 8 March 2018).

Resource 13: Living Together: Muslims in a Changing World

Rahat Zaidi

The goal of this resource is to help teachers and students understand one another and appreciate similarities within apparent differences. It is designed to engage students in critical and creative thinking and help them develop an understanding of other viewpoints and perspectives. Topics include Islamic scientific, artistic and historical contributions and histories, and cultural traditions in food, dress and spiritual practice. The activities included throughout the resource include a wide range of engaging, grade-appropriate individual and group tasks. See http://living-together.ca/index.shtml.

Resource 14: Homework for Newcomers

Paula Markus and Tobin Zikmanis

Homework for newcomers is defined here as meaningful and purposeful learning tasks and activities that originate in the school and extend to the home and the community. Such three-way learning gives newcomers a voice, helps them integrate into their new school environments and links their three worlds: home, school and community. It builds on their prior knowledge, brings them into the curriculum, and helps them learn the school language, grow bilingually, make friends, feel competent and experience success.

Getting started

As you plan learning tasks be mindful of newcomers'

- interests, skills and abilities;
- home language or languages;
- literacy skills and levels;
- home literacy practices;
- prior schooling;
- homework experiences;
- the homework expectations of parents; and
- opportunity for community participation and engagement.

5 Homework suggestions

As you read the five homework suggestions provided here, think of how they can be modified or extended to match newcomers' prior school experiences, language proficiency and understanding of literacy.

(1) Family talk

Encourage newcomer families to talk with their children. Families with limited proficiency in the school language can support their children by talking to them in the home language about their new school, their classmates, their teachers and school activities and happenings. According to Rubin *et al.* (2012), such ongoing family talk is important for five reasons:

- It increases children's home language vocabularies.
- It helps them learn the school language.
- It allows for transfer of concepts into the school language.
- It positively affects their academic achievement.
- It bridges the home and the school.

(2) Personal narratives and identity texts

Invite newcomers to talk about their interests and experiences. Encourage them to work with same-language classmates (with partners or in groups), choose topics that are important to them, engage their families, share ideas and, using self-selected materials and age-appropriate digital tools, prepare projects to share with the class, their families and the school community. Examples of narratives and identity texts can be found in Chapter 2 (LAP teachers rely on technology: Tell me your story).

(3) Extending newcomers' classroom tasks

(a) Share dual-language books (in the school language) in the classroom and then send them home, inviting families to read them with children in the home language.
(b) Invite parents to create bilingual word lists by translating classroom word lists into home languages.

(c) Create a classroom website where newcomers can showcase their projects and class contributions.

(d) Use the *Home Oral Language Activities* (HOLA) programme,[5] a language and literacy resource for newcomer families, to help young children develop their home language vocabulary, improve their communication skills and engage with literacy.

(e) Homework clubs are a 'tried and true' support for older newcomers who find themselves with a double challenge: learning the school language and managing the curriculum. Homework clubs can be organized in a number of contexts. In the classroom, newcomers can find support from teachers and be paired with homework buddies. In the school and the community, teachers, parents and volunteers can provide homework coaching and tutoring.

(4) Documenting and sharing learning

Encourage newcomers to record their school and home learning tasks. This can take the form of a self-created (or purchased) notebook or journal or it can be prepared electronically as an e-journal. Ensure that newcomers take the lead in their journal tasks. Discuss and provide choices and options, such as length of entries, language choice, images, photos, collaboration with classmates, contributions from families and communities, sharing practices, confidentiality and storage.

(5) Book time: School, home and library

Add a book time to your daily classroom schedule. Vary the book-sharing space: classroom, school library, public library. Build a classroom reading collection that includes dual-language and multilingual books and newspapers. Invite same-language children, other teachers and family members to share books in home languages.

Resource 15: Five More LAP Activities

(1) 'Throw your tooth on the roof: Tooth traditions from around the world'

Beeler, S. (2003) *Throw Your Tooth on the Roof: Tooth Traditions from Around the World.* Boston, MA: HMH Books for Young Readers.

In a Grade 2 Toronto classroom, a child's loose tooth turned into a high-interest event. Children gathered around to view the wiggly tooth, asked questions and shared experiences of what to do to receive a reward for the tooth once it fell out. Following up on this interest, the teacher created a series of activities. She first engaged the children in a discussion about loose teeth. Most were familiar with the tooth fairy and the joy of waking up to a find an under-the-pillow surprise in exchange for a tooth.

At this point the teacher asked: '*Do you think the tooth fairy visits children all over the world?*' While most children nodded, some remained uncertain. At this point the teacher introduced the book entitled *Throw Your Tooth on the Roof: Tooth Traditions from Around the World*. Following the excited response to the funny title, she explained the word 'tradition' and then proceeded to read the story.

In this delightful story, children from countries on each continent explain what they do when they lose a tooth. Not all children wait for the tooth fairy. In Chile or Costa Rica, parents transform children's teeth into charms, whereas children in Venezuela put their teeth under the pillow and wait for a mouse to bring money. In Botswana, children throw their teeth onto the roof. In Afghanistan they drop their teeth down mouse holes, and in Egypt they fling their teeth at the sun!

Follow-up activities

(a) Create a multilingual word list: translations of the word *tooth* and *teeth* in children's home languages.
(b) Teeth facts and terminology: baby, milk, temporary, primary, permanent and names of teeth.
(c) Discussion of tooth traditions in children's cultures. Interviews with parents and grandparents who report on their childhood lost tooth experiences (see Box).
(d) Writing tooth stories.
(e) Visit from a dentist followed by a discussion about dental hygiene and the care of teeth.

In Nepal if your tooth falls out we hide it because if a crow finds it you won't grow a new one. So that is why we hide it under the soil – so that the crow can't get to it.

Once my baby tooth has fallen out I will throw it in the garden. I ask my parents what did you do with your lost teeth. And they said they buried them in the hills.

In our country we throw lost teeth on the roof or in the hills.

Back home in our country we take our tooth put it in a mouse hole. The mouses strong teeth swaps with your teeth.

One day when I was brushing my teeth a baby tooth fell out and I got scared because there was lots of blood coming out from my mouth. Then I washed my teeth. After that I went to bed. I put my baby teeth under my pillow. In the morning when I got up I saw a doller under my pillow. I even thought that a tooth fairy came and gave me a doller.

A long time ago my grandparents put a baby tooth under the goats footprints and they covered it with sand. My grandparents prayed that they will get a baby tooth like a goat. By mistake if they put the baby tooth under the cows footprint they will get a big tooth like a cow. Finally these are the tradition that my family uses.

(2) A multilingual calendar

When a Canadian Grade 2 teacher saw that the morning calendar discussion (month, year, day, weather, planned events) was becoming routine, she invited the children to think of ways to energize it. They responded enthusiastically with suggestions and ideas. The consensus was to transform the calendar into a multilingual tool where information would be presented in English and also in home languages. This was followed by discussions of translations (names of days, weeks, months, seasons and numbers), and the collaborative preparation of the November multilingual calendar (see Figure 5.3).

(3) Dressing for winter

Some newcomers experience cold weather for the first time when they arrive in their new countries.

Activities to help newcomers understand and enjoy winter in all its magic and fun!

(a) *Reading about snow and winter*
Here are three classics to share with children:

Briggs, R. (1970) *The Snowman*. New York: Random House.
Keats, E.J. (1962) *The Snowy Day*. New York: Viking.
Neitzel, S. and Winslow Parker, N. (1989) *The Jacket I Wear in the Snow*. New York: Greenwillow Books.

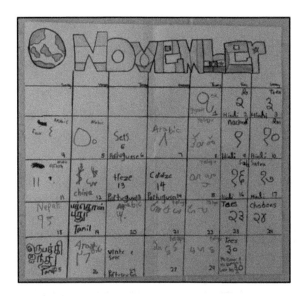

Figure 5.3 Multilingual calendar

The school librarian and an internet search will provide you with more winter-themed books. Also, many narrated winter stories, some in bilingual versions (English and Spanish, Russian, Armenian and French) are available on YouTube for group or individual listening and viewing.

(b) *Winter word lists*

Ask children to make a list of winter words. Once the class list is complete, invite the children to categorize the words thematically (clothing, activities, drinks) and also into parts of speech: nouns, adjectives and verbs. Finally, invite newcomers to provide home language translations for the words.

(c) *Climate and seasons*

Invite newcomers and same-language classmates to share information about the seasons and the climate in their countries of origin. Provide choice of language, materials and mode of sharing or presenting.

(d) *Winter holidays and celebrations*

The winter months are a time of celebration. With the help of families and the internet, list all the different holidays and special days celebrated in the winter months. Encourage the children to work together to prepare short presentations about their special days.

(e) *Winter wordsearch*

Children love word searches. Create your own winter word search using this template: http://tools.atozteacherstuff.com/word-search-maker/wordsearch.php. Also use the winter word search from Scholastic: https://www.scholastic.com/parents/kids-activities-and-printables/printables/reading-worksheets/winter-word-search.html.

(4) Postage stamps

Postage stamps are an important resource in the multilingual classroom. Their declining use (due to electronic communication) should not stop teachers from introducing children to the world of philately or stamp study and collection. Postage stamps symbolize national identity and have the potential to teach everyone (not just children) a great deal about geography, history, world currencies and cultures, art and design.

Discussion topics include:

- history of postage stamps and mail services;
- first postage stamp (England, 1840, with an image of Queen Victoria);
- The Postal Museum in London;
- study of stamps, stamp collection and postal history;
- tools philatelists use;
- images and words on postage stamps;
- postage stamp series and themes;
- cost and value of stamps; and
- how to remove stamps from envelopes.

Postage stamp activities

(a) Postage stamps from my country, the country of my parents and grandparents
(b) Creating school, class and personal stamps: choosing design, images and value
(c) Class postage stamp album
(d) Class post office
(e) Stamp collector's club

Resources

https://postalhistoryfoundation.org/yes-program/hobby-and-fun-resources/
    stamp-collecting-starter-kits/.
https://www.postalmuseum.org/christmas-2018/#.
Obojski, R. (2004) *A First Stamp Album for Beginners*. New York: Dover.

(5) Languages of the World

Davis, W., Handicott, B. and Pak, K. (2016) *Hello Atlas*. New York: Wide Eyed Editions.

> 'Whatever corner of the world you're reading from, the *Hello Atlas* is an invitation to explore the great diversity of language and experience the gift that it gives: hope, inspiration and a promise for the future.'

This activity invites all children, not only newcomers, to explore the global language landscape and better understand languages. The *Hello Atlas* is a valuable resource that will help guide this activity. It features a sampling of greetings and 'conversational overtures' in languages spoken on each of the seven continents: Africa, Antarctica, Asia, Europe, North America, Australasia or Oceania and South America. In the Foreword, Professor Wade Davis, a Canadian ethnobotanist and explorer, reminds readers that each and every language is a treasure trove of knowledge, experience, culture, wisdom, poetry and song. The introduction, entitled 'How to use this book', together with an accompanying free app (downloadable for iOS and Android, which provides audio versions of the phrases, recorded by native speakers) will help readers navigate the seven attractive and beautifully illustrated sections. The 'Further phrases' (found at the end of the book) will help children extend their study and exploration of languages.

Tips for exploring world languages
(1) Language talk

Use the following topics to engage children in a discussion about language: language names, language families, language distribution and language status (official and non-official). See Language Fact Sheet (Chapter 4: How many languages are there in the world?)

(2) Hello Atlas: Introduction and discovery

Briefly introduce the *Hello Atlas* and step back, inviting children to discover the book on their own or in small groups.

(3) Hello Atlas: Discussion and response

Consider the following as you plan a *Hello Atlas* group discussion:

- children's home languages;
- languages missing from the *Hello Atlas*;
- the continents (names, geographical location, main features); and
- writing systems, alphabets, text directionality and pronunciation.

(4) Classroom *Hello Atlas*

Invite children to take the lead on this class project. Help them to them to:

(a) Document the languages spoken by everyone in the class.
(b) Create a multidisciplinary project by making connections to language, geography, maths, music, history and technology. Use the flowchart in Figure 5.4 as a starting point, adding topics to the subject areas and creating additional subject connections.

(5) School *Hello Atlas*

This project showcases the languages of the entire school community. With contributions from each classroom, the School Hello Atlas is displayed during school events, such as open houses, holiday concerts or parent-teacher interviews.

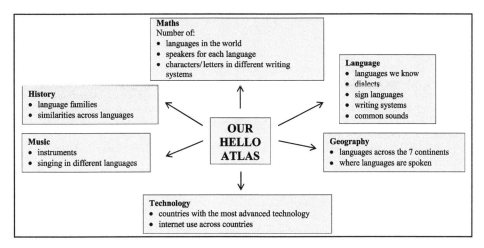

Figure 5.4 Flowchart: Our Hello Atlas

Consider this ...

(1) Review the six building blocks on the LAP guide and position your multilingual work. Share your LAP journey with your colleagues. When did you begin your multilingual teaching? What are the next steps?

(2) Organize a professional book club. Discuss meeting times, places, guest authors and readings.

(3) Organize a multilingual book drive in your school. Engage the children in planning, advertising and collecting books.

(4) Ask the school music teacher to add songs in children's home languages to her programme. Also, invite families to come to your classroom to share songs from their cultures.

(5) Organize a 'Languages Matter' evening in your school. Invite families to share ideas about bilingualism, home languages and literacies. Use the 'Language of the Home: Foundation for Success' DVD to generate discussion.

Notes

(1) See https://global.oup.com/education/content/primary/series/international-english/oiey-the-glitterlings/?region=international.

(2) See http://zmi-koeln.de/.

(3) Halton is a regional municipality located in Southern Ontario, Canada.

(4) See https://hangouts.google.com/?hl=it.

(5) The Home Oral Language Activities (HOLA) programme is a book bag programme developed in 2010 by the Toronto District School Boards (TDSB). Intended for kindergarten and Grade 1 children, HOLA can be used at home and in the classroom. The kit includes language and literacy activities and thematic books in 12 languages (Arabic, Bengali, Chinese, English, Farsi, Gujarati, Korean, Somali, Spanish, Tamil, Urdu and Vietnamese). Contact curriculumdocs@tdsb.on.ca to purchase the HOLA kit.

References

Abbott, M. (2002) Using music to promote L2 learning among adult learners. *TESOL Journal* 11 (1), 10–17.

Alisaari, J. (2015) Laulaminen paikallissijojen harjoittelun menetelmänä S2-opetuksessa. In M. Kauppinen, M. Rautiainen and M. Tarnanen (eds) *Elävä ainepedagogiikka. Ainedidaktiikan symposium Jyväskylässä 13–14.2.2014. Suomen ainedidaktisen tutkimusseuran julkaisuja* (pp. 210–224). Ainedidaktisia Tutkimuksia 9. Jyväskylä: Suomen ainedidaktinen tutkimusseurary. See https://helda.helsinki.fi/handle/10138/154156.

Campbell, P. (2010) *Songs in their Heads: Music and its Meaning in Children's Lives* (2nd edn). New York: Oxford University Press.

Corbeil, M., Trehub, S.E. and Peretz, I. (2016) Singing delays the onset of infant distress. *Infancy* 21 (3), 373–391.

Domoney, L. and Harris, S. (1993) Justified and ancient: Pop music in EFL classrooms. *ELT Journal* 47 (3), 234–241. doi.org/10.1093/elt/47.3.234

Dunbar, R.I.M., Kaskatis, K., MacDonald, I. and Barra, V. (2012) Performance of music elevates pain threshold and positive affect: Implications for the evolutionary function of music. *Evolutionary Psychology* 10 (4), 688–702.

Ferazzi, K. (2014) *Never Eat Alone*. New York: Penguin.

Hakkarainen, K., Bollström-Huttunen, M., Pyysalo Riikka and Lonka, K. (2005) *Tutkiva oppiminen käytännössä: Opettajan matkaopas*. Helsinki: WSOY.

Ilari, B. (2016) Music in the early years: Pathways into the social world. *Research Studies in Music Education* 38 (1), 23–39.

James, C.J. (ed.) (1985) *Foreign Language Proficiency in the Classroom and Beyond*. ACTFL Foreign Language Education Series. Lincolnwood, IL: National Textbook Company.

Kilgour, A.R., Jakobson, L.S. and Cuddy, L.L. (2000) Music training and rate of presentation as mediators of text and song recall. *Memory and Cognition* 28, 700–710.

Krashen, S.D. (2009) *Principles and Practice in Second Language Acquisition*. Los Angeles, CA: University of Southern California. See www.sdkrashen.com/content/books/principles_and_practice.pdf (accessed 22 February 2018).

Lake, R. (2003) Enhancing acquisition through music. *Journal of the Imagination in Language Learning* 7, 98–107.

Legg, R. (2009) Using music to accelerate language learning: An experimental study. *Research in Education* 82, 1–12. doi:10.7227/RIE.82.1

Lems, K. (2005) Music works: Music for adult English language learners. *New Directions for Adult and Continuing Education* 107, 13–21. doi:10.1002/ace.185

Malloch, S. and Trevarthen, C. (eds) (2008) *Communicative Musicality*. New York: Oxford University Press.

Rubin, R., Abrego, M.H. and Sutterby, J.A. (2012) *Engaging the Families of ELLs: Ideas, Resources and Activities*. New York: Eye on Education.

Spychiger, M., Patry, J., Lauper, G., Simmermann, E. and Weber, E. (1995) Does more music teaching lead to a better social climate? In R. Olechowski and G. Khan-Svik (eds) *Experimental Research on Teaching and Learning* (pp. 322–336). Frankfurt: Peter Lang.

Terhart, H. and von Dewitz, N. (2018) Newly arrived migrant students in German schools: Exclusive and inclusive structures and practices. *European Educational Research Journal* 17 (2), 290–304.

Wiltermuth, S.S. and Heath, C. (2009) Synchrony and cooperation. *Psychological Science* 20 (1), 1–5. doi:10.1111/j.1467-9280.2008.02253.x

In Closing …

My five-year fact-finding LAP journey has come to an end. During my many interactions with children, teachers and families, I saw LAP in all its excitement and richness. I witnessed creative teaching and busy, vibrant learning. I saw understanding and pride as newcomers, bilinguals and monolingual children worked together and shared their learning. In classrooms, auditoriums and libraries, I saw families opening up the world to children by sharing their knowledge, their languages and their literacies.

I visited schools where home languages were seen, heard, used and included in the curriculum. I saw some teachers take first LAP steps and others transform their classrooms into multilingual leaning spaces, abuzz with languages and literacies. I saw children reach out to newcomers, help each other and learn from each other. I observed them using their home languages and listening to stories and narratives read in languages they did not understand. What they did understand, however, is that these are the languages of their classmates and friends – and that they matter.

5 **Take-away Messages**

This book ends in the same way it started: with the number five. I offer the reader five take-away messages. Read them with your colleagues and discuss and share the ideas. Keep the messages in mind as you travel your LAP journey and advocate for multilingual teaching.

(1) LAP is for everyone!

Five years ago, I presented LAP as an inclusive and effective way to integrate and support young 'immigrant' children. However, after my five-year fact-finding journey, I know that LAP is far, far more than an instructional practice for one specific group of children. The enthusiastic response to LAP from *all* children shows that this kind of teaching is an invaluable enrichment for everyone. It is the instructional practice of the 21st century and the 'way to go' in schools and classrooms filled with children, families and teachers from different language backgrounds.

(2) The LAP glass

The LAP glass is filling up and looking good. The profiles, journeys and actions presented in Chapter 3 show us that teachers across Canada, Europe and the Nordic countries are responding to changing school populations and matching their pedagogy to the lived experiences of all children. Following Howard's (2007) mantra, 'as diversity grows, so must we', they are reviewing and retooling their practice, collaborating with education researchers, extending their understanding of bilingualism and diversity, developing multilingual resources and reaching out to families.

Jim Cummins, an international authority on language and literacy development and pedagogy, believes that multilingual teaching has reached a 'tipping point'. This means that:

* multilingual teaching has reached a critical point;
* inclusive practice is spreading and evolving;
* linguistically diverse populations are becoming a priority for schools, educational researchers, curriculum writers and policy makers; and
* teachers are engaging in professional understanding and inquiry, moving away from assimilative and supportive practices, rethinking and retooling their teaching and adopting multilingual pedagogy.

(3) Much remains to be done

A reality check shows us that the LAP glass is not quite full. This means that the robust multilingual teaching and learning portrayed in this book is not the whole story. What does this mean? It means that there are teachers who, for personal, professional and curricular reasons (Chumak-Horbatsch, 2017), remain hesitant and unwilling to align their practice with the linguistic diversity of their classrooms.

This reality is a reminder for all LAP teachers to reach out to colleagues who are hesitant or unsure. Here are suggestions for advocating for multilingual teaching:

* reach out to colleagues who are new to LAP;
* plan team teaching sessions;
* seek funds to support and fund multilingual projects;
* offer to do demonstration multilingual lessons;
* share ideas, resources and teaching strategies;
* engage in professional discussion; and
* organize and attend multilingual workshops and conferences.

(4) The importance of understanding: 'This is what I do, and this is why I do it.'

The LAP tree (Chapter 1, Figure 1.1) serves as a reminder that multilingual teaching is not an activity-driven and short-lived experience. Rather, it is a commitment to teaching with the understanding that LAP activities and projects are directly in line with and grounded in learning and bilingualism theories.

An understanding of the roots of the LAP tree will strengthen and fortify its branches and leaves. Familiarity with the learning and bilingualism theories that explain LAP will reinforce LAP actions, enabling teachers to sustain and justify their multilingual work and develop the professional confidence to say: 'This is what I do, and this is why I do it.'

Serving as a guiding light, the LAP tree helps teachers keep the following at the forefront of their teaching:

- include everyone;
- provide equal opportunity for all to participate and learn;
- link home and school experiences;
- build on prior knowledge;
- ensure that classroom experiences are relevant and meaningful for all children;
- engage, challenge and support all children;
- encourage children to take control of their learning;
- encourage questioning and critical thinking;
- create spaces for home languages and literacies; and
- encourage children to use their entire language repertoire to learn and discover.

(5) Do it your way

The adoption of LAP is a personal and professional journey which varies across teachers, learning contexts, school populations and countries. Instructional practice reflection, review, resolve, change and commitment will not be the same for all teachers. The 'right' way to embark on the LAP journey is to do it 'your way'.

If you are new to multilingual teaching or if you have taken first steps but feel uncertain about how to move forward, go back to the LAP guide. The six building blocks will help you position your multilingual work and give you a sense of direction. Connect with seasoned LAP teachers and reread the LAP profiles found in Chapter 3. Review the hidden part of the LAP tree and solidify your understanding of the underlying theories.

Final Thoughts

A multilingual movement

This is an exciting time to be a teacher. Changing school populations and linguistic diversity have sparked an evolution in teaching. They have challenged teachers, refocused thinking and learning from the local to the global, shifted instructional practice from monolingual to multilingual, and transformed schools into inclusive and vibrant learning hubs.

A multilingual community of practice

I have been thinking about my next LAP journey. Running in High Park, past confused robins, prematurely returned to snowy and frigid Toronto, I found the answer.

Thinking about the countless practitioners and teachers I interacted with during my LAP fact-finding journey, I know that the time has come to bring the multilingual teaching community together. And so, then and there, I decided to develop an online multilingual community of practice. This social learning and sharing space will be linked to my current website: https://www.ryerson.ca/mylanguage/. It will provide professionals and practitioners who share a commitment and a passion for multilingual teaching with the opportunity to connect across geographic boundaries, share experiences and knowledge, engage in professional learning, collaborate and learn from each other and strengthen their commitment to multilingual teaching.

And the goal of developing an online multilingual community of practice?

To fill the LAP glass to the brim!

References

Chumak-Horbatsch, R. (2017) Instructional practice with young bilingual learners: A Canadian profile. In N. Cabrera and B. Leyendecker (eds) *Handbook on Positive Development of Minority Children*. Dordrecht: Springer.

Howard, G.R. (2007) Responding to changing demographics: As diversity grows, so must we. *Educational Leadership* 64 (6), 16–22.

Appendix

(1) Professional Reading List
(2) Children's Books
(3) Books and Websites to Share with Families
(4) The Glitterlings
(5) The Best of All Worlds – Le meilleur monde imaginable

(1) Professional Reading List

Here is a list of readings for you to explore in your book club. Use it as a starting point to build your own reading list.

Baker, C. (2000) *The Care and Education of Young Bilinguals: An Introduction for Professionals.* Clevedon: Multilingual Matters.

Beststart.org (2014) *When Children Speak More than One Language.* Ontario: Best Start Resource Centre/Government of Ontario. See https://www.beststart.org/resources/hlthy_chld_dev/BSRC_When_Families_Speak_fnl.pdf (accessed 17 February 2018).

Chumak-Horbatsch, R. (2012) *Linguistically Appropriate Practice: Working with A Guide for Working with Young Immigrant Children.* Toronto: University of Toronto Press.

CMAS (2015) *Caring for Syrian Refugee Children: A Program Guide for Welcoming Young Children and Their Families.* Toronto: CMAS. See https://cmascanada.ca//wp-content/uploads/2015/12/Supporting_Refugees/Caring%20for%20Syrian%20Refugee%20Children-final.pdf (accessed 21 March 2019).

Coelho, E. (2012) *Language and Learning in Multilingual Classrooms: A Practical Approach.* Bristol: Multilingual Matters.

Cummins, J. (2001) *Bilingual Children's Mother Tongue: Why is it Important for Education?* See http://www.lavplu.eu/central/bibliografie/cummins_eng.pdf (accessed 21 March 2019).

Cummins, J. (2007) Rethinking monolingual instructional strategies in multilingual classrooms. *Canadian Journal of Applied Linguistics* 10 (2), 221–240.

Cummins, J. and Early, M. (2015) *Big Ideas for Expanding Minds: Teaching English Language Learners Across the Curriculum*, Toronto: Rubicon, Pearson.

Cummins, J. and Persad, R. (2014) Teaching through a multilingual lens: The evolution of EAL policy and practice in Canada. *Education Matters* 2, 3–40. See https://globalconversationsinliteracy.files.wordpress.com/2014/08/cummins2014.pdf (accessed 21 March 2019).

Cummins, J., Bismilla, V., Chow, P., Cohen, S., Giampapa, F., Leoni, L., Sandhu, P. and Sastri, P. (2005) Affirming identity in multilingual classrooms. *Educational Leadership* 63 (1), 38–43.

García, O. (2009) Emergent bilinguals and TESOL: What's in a name? *TESOL Quarterly* 43 (2), 322–326.

Kenner, C. (2007) *Home Pages: Literacy Links for Bilingual Children*. London: Trentham Books.

Kenner, C. and Ruby, M. (2012) *Interconnecting Worlds: Teacher Partnerships for Bilingual Learning*. London: Institute of Education Press.

Krulatz, A., Dahl, A. and Flognfeldt, M.E. (eds) (2018) *Enacting Multilingualism: From Research to Teaching Practice in the English Classroom*. Oslo: Cappellen Damm Akademisk.

Maybank, M. (1999) The need to nurture home languages in the classroom. *International Journal of Primary, Elementary and Early Years Education* 27 (2), 10–15.

Rader, D. (2018) *Teaching and Learning for Intercultural Understanding: Engaging Young Hearts and Minds*. New York: Routledge.

Schwarzer, D., Haywood, A. and Lorenzen, C. (2003) Fostering multiliteracy in a linguistically diverse classroom: How does a monolingual teacher support linguistic diversity in a classroom of children who speak many different native languages? *Language Arts* 80 (6), 453–460.

Stebih, I. (2003) Language minority children walk in two worlds. *Canadian Children* 28, 28–34.

(2) Children's Books and Websites

Picture books about refugee and newcomer children

Agosin, M. (2014) *I Lived on Butterfly Hill*. New York: Atheneum Books for Young Readers.

Ajmera, M., Nakassis, M. and Pon, C. (2009) *Faith*. Watertown, MA: Charlesbridge.

Aktar, N. and Attard, E. (1999) *Samira's Eid*. London: Mantra.

Aliki (1999) *Marianthe's Story*. New York: Greenwillow Books.

Ashley, B. (1993) *Cleversticks*. New York: Harper Collins.

Barkow, H. and Lamont, P. (2006) *Tom and Sofia Start School*. London: Mantra.

Beckwith, K. (2005) *Playing War*. Gardiner, ME: Tilbury House.

Booth, A. (2016) *Refuge*. New York: Little, Brown.

Brown, E. (2003) *Handa's Hen*. London: Mantra.

Buitrago, J. (2015) *Two White Rabbits*. Toronto: Groundwood Books.

Bunting, E. (2006) *One Green Apple*. New York: Clarion Books.

Camp, L. (2008) *Keeping up with Cheetah*. London: Mantra.

Campbell, R. (1982) *Dear Zoo*. New York: Four Winds Press.

Carden, M. and Cappellini, M. (eds) (1997) *I Am of Two Places: Children's Poetry*. Crystal Lake, IL: Rigby.

Choi, Y. (2001) *The Name Jar*. New York: Alfred A. Knopf.

Curtis, C. and Jay, A. (2004) *I Took the Moon for a Walk*. Cambridge, MA: Barefoot Books.

Daly, N. (2000) *Jamela's Dress*. London: Francis Lincoln.

Danticat, E. (2015) *Mama's Nightingale: A Story of Immigration and Separation*. New York: Dial Books for Young Readers.

English, K. (2000) *Speak English for Us, Marisol!* Morton Grove, IL: Albert Whitman.

Garay, L. (1997) *The Long Road*. Toronto: Tundra Books.

Garland, S. (1997) *The Lotus Seed*. San Diego, CA: Harcourt Brace.

Garland, S. (2013) *Azzi in Between*. London: Frances Lincoln Children's.

Harter, D. (2006) *Walking Through the Jungle*. Cambridge, MA: Barefoot Books.

Heide, F.P. (1992) *Sami and the Time of Troubles*. New York: Clarion Books.

Herrera, J. (2000) *The Upside Down Boy/El nino de cabeza*. San Francisco, CA: Children's Book Press.

Hoffmann, M. (2002) *The Colour of Home*. New York: Dial Books for Young Readers.

Hyde, H. (2010) *Feivel's Flying Horses*. Minneapolis, MN: Kar-Ben.

Jimenez, F. (1998) *La mariposa*. Boston, MA: Houghton Mifflin.

Keefer, J. (2000) *Anna's Goat*. Victoria, BC: Orca Books.

Khan, R. (2008) *Coming to Canada*. Toronto: Groundwood Books.

Kim, P. (2013) *Here I Am*. North Mankato, MN: Picture Window Books.

Kobald, I. (2015) *My Two Blankets*. Boston, MA: Houghton Mifflin Harcourt.

Krebs, L. (2003) *We All Went on Safari: A Counting Journey Through Tanzania*. Cambridge, MA: Barefoot Books.

Kroll, V. (1995) *Jaha and Jamil Went Down the Hill: An African Mother Goose*. Waterdown, MA: Charlesbridge.

Kubler, A. (2001) *The Wheels on the Bus Go Round and Round*. London: Mantra.

Kubler, A. (2006) *Head, Shoulders, Knees and Toes*. London: Mantra.

Kubler, A. (2010) *Row, Row, Row your Boat*. London: Mantra.

Kuntz, D. and Shrodes, A. (2017) *Lost and Found Cat: The True Story of Kunkush's Incredible Journey*. New York: Crown Books for Young Readers.

Levine, E. (1989) *I Hate English!* New York: Scholastic.

Martin, B. (1983) *Brown Bear, Brown Bear, What Do You See?* New York: Henry Holt.

McQuinn, A. (2008) *My Friend Jamal*. Toronto: Annick Press.

Miller, E. (1999) *Just Like Home/Como en mi tierra*. Morton Grove, IL: Albert Whitman.

Mills, D. (2003) *The Wibbly Wobbly Tooth*. London: Mantra.

Mitchell, P. (2004) *Petar's Song*. London: Francis Lincoln Children's Books.

Mobin-Uddin, A. (2005) *My Name is Bilal*. Homesdale, PA: Boyds Mills Press.

Munsch, R. (1995) *From Far Away*. Toronto: Annick Press.

Nobisso, J. (2002) *In English of Course*. New York: Gingerbread House.

Norac, C. (2004) *My Daddy is a Giant*. London: Mantra.

Nunn, D. (2012) *Arabic: Languages of the World*. Chicago, IL: Heinemann Library.

Pak, S. (2002) *A Place to Grow*. New York: Scholastic.

Pak, S. (2003) *Sumi's First Day of School Ever*. New York: Viking.

Park, F. and Park, G. (2002) *Goodbye, 382 Shin Dang Dong*. Washington, DC: National Geographic Society.

Pinkney, A.D. (2014) *The Red Pencil*. New York: Little, Brown.

Recorvits, H. (2003) *My Name is Yoon*. New York: Farrar, Straus & Giroux.

Robert, N. (2002) *The Swirling Hijaab*. London: Mantra.

Robert, N. (2005) *Welcome to the World Baby*. London: Mantra.

Robinson, A. and Young, A. (2010) *Gervelie's Journey: A Refugee Diary*. London: Francis Lincoln.

Rosenberg, L. (1999) *The Silence in the Mountains*. New York: Orchard Books.

Ruurs, M. (2016) *Stepping Stones*. Victoria, BC: Orca Books.

Sanna, F. (2016) *The Journey*. London: Flying Eye Books.

Shulevitz, U. (2008) *How I Learned Geography*. New York: Farrar, Straus & Giroux.

Sibley O'Brien, A. (2015) *I'm New Here*. Watertown, MA: Charlesbridge.

Simon, R. (2015) *Oskar and the Eight Blessings*. New York: Roaring Book Press.

Sis, P. (2000) *Madlenka*. Vancouver: Douglas & McIntyre.

Tan, S. (2006) *The Arrival*. New York: Arthur A. Levine Books.

Thien, M. (2001) *The Chinese Violin*. Vancouver: Whitecap Books.

Wilkes, S. (1994) *One Day We Had to Run! Refugee Children Tell their Stories in Words and Paintings*. London: Evans Brothers.

Williams, K. (2009) *My Name is Sangoel*. Grand Rapids, MI: Eerdmans Books for Young Readers.

Williams, K. and Mohammed, K. (2007) *Four Feet, Two Sandals*. Grand Rapids, MI: Eerdmans Books for Young Readers.

Williams, M. (2005) *Brothers in Hope: The Story of the Lost Boys of Sudan*. New York: Lee & Low Books.

Yaccarino, D. (2011) *All the Way to America*. New York: Alfred A. Knopf.

Young, R. (2016) *Teacup*. New York: Dial Books for Young Readers.

Books about language

Bullard, L. (2015) *My Language, Your Language*. Minneapolis, MN: Millbrook Press.
Cooper, K. (1992) *Why Do You Speak as You Do? A Guide to World Languages*. New York: Walker.
Cox, B.S. (1995) *Who Talks Funny? A Book about Languages for Kids*. North Haven, CT: Linnet Books.
Isabella, J. (2013) *Chitchat: Celebrating the World's Languages*. Toronto: Kids Can Press.
Isadora, R. (2010) *Say Hello!* New York: G.P. Putnam's Sons.
Katz, K. (2006) *Can You Say Peace?* New York: Henry Holt.
Kutschbach, D. (2014) *Art: A World of Words. First Paintings – First Words in 12 Languages*. New York: Prestel.
Park, L.S. (2009) *Mung-Mung: A Foldout Book of Animal Sounds*. Watertown, MA: Charlesbridge.
Stojic, M. (2002) *Hello World! Greetings in 42 Languages Around the Globe*. Toronto: Scholastic.
Wellington, M. and Leventhal, D. (1994) *What Is Your Language?* Boston, MA: Dutton Penguin.

Books about grandparents

Crystal, B. (2006) *Grandpa's Little One*. New York: Harper Collins.
DePaola, T. (1981) *Now One Foot, Now the Other*. New York: Putnam.
DePaola, T. (1998) *Nana Upstairs and Nana Downstairs*. New York: Putnam.
Dorros, A. (1991) *Abuela*. New York: Dutton Children's Books.
Johnson, A. (1990) *When I Am Old With You*. New York: Orchard Books.
Juster, N. (2005) *Hello, Goodbye Window*. New York: Hyperion Books for Children.
Lamarche, J. (2000) *The Raft*. New York: Lothrop, Lee & Sheppard.
Lloyd-James, S. and Emberley, M. (2008) *The Ultimate Guide to Grandmas and Grandpas!* New York: Harper Collins.
Martin, M.P. (1971) *Annie and the Old One*. Boston, MA: Little, Brown.
Mayer, M. (1983) *Just Grandma and Me*. New York: Golden Press.
Minarik, H.E. (1961) *Little Bear's Visit*. New York: Harper and Row.
Rylant, C. (1982) *When I Was Young in the Mountains*. New York: Dutton.
Spyri, J. (2006) *Heidi*. New York: Sterling.

Multilingual digital book collections

Here are 10 websites where you will find video- and audio-clips, dual-language books for sale, and also free-access books. The website addresses were accessed on 8 January 2018.

¡Colorín Colorado!

http://www.colorincolorado.org/booklist/refugee-experience-books-children

This is a popular American website for teachers and families of English language learners (ELLs) in Grades PreK to12. It includes free research-based information, activities and advice to parents, schools and communities. Where does the name *Colorín Colorado* come from? Just ask a Spanish speaker and you will discover that this phrase is often heard at the end of stories in Spanish-speaking countries: '¡Y *Colorín Colorado, este cuento se ha acabado!*' or '¡Y *Colorín Colorado, este cuento se ha terminado!*' (Colorín Colorado, the story has ended!). There is no equivalent in English, but the phrase is similar to 'The End' or '… and they lived happily ever after'.

YouTube

https://www.youtube.com/

YouTube is a goldmine for children's multilingual stories. Just type in the name of the language you need in order to access stories, songs and more.

Reading A–Z

https://www.readinga-z.com/worldlanguages/

This website offers a wealth of books to support children's learning in Spanish, French, Polish, Ukrainian, Vietnamese and English.

Edition bi:libri

http://www.edition-bilibri.com/

Edition bi:libri specializes in children's bilingual books. The stories depict universal themes such as otherness, belonging, friendship and individuality.

You Are Special

http://www.youarespecial.com/

You Are Special specializes in dual-language and multicultural children's books that combine English with over 50 other languages.

Language Lizard

https://www.languagelizard.com/

This website offers dual-language books, CDs and posters in English with a choice of over 40 languages, including both popular and less commonly taught languages. The innovative and creative stories will expose children to world cultures and traditions.

Who I Am Children's World Library

http://www.whoiam.at/who-i-am-childrens-world-library.html

The Who I Am Children's World Library consists of over 5200 books, 600 music books and audiobooks, and 300 films in German, as well as 4200 titles in over 40 different languages. In addition to its international collection of literature, the collaborative project 'repatriated' children's literature by making languages accessible that are not recognized as a national language anywhere in the world. These languages include Pashto, Dari, Romani, Chechen and Kurdish.

International Children's Digital Library (ICDL)

http://en.childrenslibrary.org/

The goal of the ICDL is to build a collection of books that represents outstanding historical and contemporary books from around the world. The foundation plans to have every culture and language represented so that every child can know and appreciate the riches of children's literature from the world community.

Unite for Literacy: Picture book abundance

http://www.uniteforliteracy.com/

This digital library provides free digital access to picture books, narrated in 35 languages.

Far Eastern Books

http://www.fareasternbooks.com/

This collection includes multilingual and dual-language books, dictionaries, DVDs, posters, maps, interactive learning CD-ROMs and talking pen books.

(3) Books and Websites to Share with Families

Books

Baker, C. (2014) *A Parents' and Teachers' Guide to Bilingualism* (4th edn). Bristol: Multilingual Matters.
Beck, A. (2016) *Maximize Your Child's Bilingual Ability: Ideas and Inspiration for Even Greater Success and Joy Raising Bilingual Kids*. Hiroshima: Bilingual Adventures.
King, K. and Mackey, A. (2007) *The Bilingual Edge: Why, When and How to Teach Your Child a Second Language*. New York: Harper Collins.
Zurer Pearson, B. (2008) *Raising a Bilingual Child. A Step-by-step Guide for Parents*. New York: Random House.

Websites and blogs

These websites were accessed 8 March 2018.

Life as a bilingual: The reality of living with two (or more) languages

https://www.psychologytoday.com/blog/life-bilingual

This blog on the Psychology Today website is maintained by François Grosjean, a world authority on bilingualism. The reader will find information on topics such as: what it means to be dominant in a language; inside the bilingual brain; and you are never too old to learn a new language.

Mylanguage.ca

https://www.ryerson.ca/mylanguage/

This website was developed by the author, Roma Chumak-Horbatsch. It provides research-based information about the importance of maintaining and protecting home languages.

On raising bilingual children

https://onraisingbilingualchildren.com/

This blog was developed by Eowyn Crisfield, a Canadian specialist in bilingualism who lives in the Netherlands. It includes guidance and suggestions for raising bilingual children.

Multilingual Living: Because global communication begins at home

http://www.multilingualliving.com/

This site was founded by Corey Heller, a parent and researcher, who is raising three bilingual children. Multilingual Living offers useful information on raising children in more than one language, including a downloadable Multilingual Living Magazine discussion forum.

Multilingual Children's Association

http://www.multilingualchildren.org/

This site has a wide variety of helpful content for parents raising children in more than one language. The site was founded by Christina Bosemark, who is originally from Sweden but now lives in San Francisco. The site brings together the information and insights she gathered while nurturing her own trilingual children.

InCulture Parent

http://www.incultureparent.com/

This 'online magazine is intended for parents raising global citizens'. The site was created by Stephanie Meade, a professional in international development and the parent of two bilingual children. It features articles on raising multicultural and multilingual children from a global perspective.

Bilingual Monkeys

http://bilingualmonkeys.com/

Bilingual Monkeys offers strategies and support to parents who are raising bilingual children. It was created by Adam Beck, an educator and parent, who has worked with hundreds of bilingual and multilingual children over the past 20 years.

(4) The Glitterlings

A group of teachers-in-training shared The Glitterlings books with five- to 10-year-old children in a linguistically diverse school. Here is what they reported in their journals.

'The Glitterlings were an instant hit!'

'Children loved the four creatures and found their adventures and antics delightful.'

'The books were presented to children in various ways. Discussions with younger children focused on books: authors, illustrators, editors, publication, printing, publishing, bookstores, libraries and caring for books. They were invited to explore the books on their own or share them with their classmates.'

'The word "polyglot" appears throughout The Glitterlings books. To the surprise and delight of the teachers-in-training, "polyglot" quickly became the "go-to" word in the classrooms. The children loved the sound of this word and formulated their own definitions. For example, a polyglot "has many tongues and eats a lot" and a polyglot "is like me, a creature who can talk in many ways". Children created their own paper and play-dough polyglots (see above) and labelled them in their home languages. Discussions about languages and language ability dominated the classrooms, hallways and the schoolyard. The children showcased their language skills (at times in delightful exaggerated ways), and asked their classmates, their teachers and visitors whether they are polyglots.'

With older children (Grades 3, 4 and 5), teachers-in-training used various resources (school librarian, internet, iPads, Google Translate and YouTube) to integrate The Glitterlings stories into subject areas such as music, geography, history, science and language arts. For example, they discussed travel and created their own passports. They danced to The Glitterlings songs, sang lullabies in different languages, created musical instruments, drew maps and created board games. They documented and compared plants, animals and weather patterns from different parts of the world. They created and shared dual-language word lists and narratives. The Glitterlings books also served as a starting point for discussions about change, belonging and acceptance. The Glitterlings books were shared with newly arrived children from Syria. Using English-Arabic dictionaries, the newcomers translated words and phrases, prepared dual-language word lists and listened to the CDs.

(5) The Best of All Worlds – Le meilleur monde imaginable

Working bilingually: home language and French

Serena is a Grade 7 French-language teacher in a Canadian school. The newcomers in her class were invited to read the stories in *Le meilleur monde imaginable* in their home language and then prepare reviews and summaries in French. She reported that this experience was meaningful and engaging to newcomers. It showed them that their home languages matter.

In addition to classroom use, Serena reported that *Le meilleur monde imaginable* was also used in a school initiative called the First Language Reading Program, where parent-volunteers shared home-language books with children.

Reading in Arabic

Gillian is a Grade 4 teacher in a linguistically diverse Canadian school. She invited an Arabic-speaking newcomer to read one of the stories in *The Best of All Worlds* in Arabic to the entire class. Gillian reported that Arabic-speaking newcomers, with little or no command of English, responded enthusiastically. They smiled, giggled and asked for a turn to read part of the story.

In the follow-up art activities, children were invited to illustrate the stories and prepare summaries in the language of their choice: home language, French, English or bilingually. The stories were shared with families, who provided help with home language writing. When asked about the experience, children reported the following:

- 'It helps me understand better when I hear it in Arabic.'
- 'I feel good because it is Arabic. I understand.'
- 'I like it most in Arabic.'
- 'I feel proud to read to the class because I speak Arabic best.'

Reading in Spanish

Gillian invited a Spanish-speaking colleague to read one of the stories in *The Best of All Worlds* in Spanish. With no Spanish-speaking children in the class, Gillian wanted to see how the children would respond to an unknown language. Here is what she observed:

- interest in an unfamiliar language was high;
- children used the illustrations to figure out the storyline;
- during the reading, children whispered to each other, trying to understand the storyline; and
- post-reading discussion centred on the language far more than on the story line: 'What language is that?' 'Where do they speak that language?' 'Do more people speak Spanish or French?'.

Following this experience, Gillian read the same story in English. In the discussion that followed, children talked about language use and language differences. They talked about what it is like to 'not understand' what is being said. They identified the feelings and emotions (loneliness, confusion and frustration) associated with learning a new language. For the follow-up to the readings, the children were invited to dramatize the story in small groups using the languages and props of their choice.

Index

computer technology 33–37, 60 *see also* apps;
    digital books/stories
Convention on the Rights of the Child (CRC) 28
Cope, B. 12
Corbeil, M. 129
country in a box 74
country profiles 115–116 *see also* cultural
    backgrounds, exploring
Creese, A. 21
critical thinking 136, 148
cultural backgrounds, exploring 71–72, 74, 87,
    115, 142–143
cultural celebrations 59, 141
cultural identity 83 *see also* multiculturalism
Cummins, J. 6, 7, 12, 15, 43, 62, 63, 147
currency 87
curriculum
    bilingual curriculum access 37
    bringing newcomers into 55–56
    inclusion of home languages 55, 60, 124–125
    Mother Tongue Syllabus 84
    participation through home languages 28, 55
    play-based curriculum 76, 89

Davidson, S. 126
Davis, W. 142
democratic participation 77
dictionary apps 33–37
digital books/stories 33, 35, 126, 135, 153–154
disengagement 32, 44, 48, 49, 104
displays of home languages 51, 63–64, 94
documenting class languages 59–60, 77, 124, 143
Domoney, L. 130
drama/performance 13
Dual Language Showcase 36, 62, 86, 128
dual-language books 8, 60, 77–78, 85–86, 90–91,
    94, 118–120, 126–128, 135, 137, 153–154
Dunbar, R.I.M. 129
dynamic assessment 31–32
dynamic bilingualism 8, 9, 13, 81

Early, M. 6
early childhood settings 47 *see also*
    kindergarten/preschool
early language intervention programmes (ELI)
    91–96
ecosystems, linguistic 21
Edition bi:libri 154
emergent bilinguals 6, 8, 45, 71, 93

endangered languages 20
engagement in learning 16, 32, 44, 60, 104–106
English as a Second Language (ESL) 47–49,
    52, 63
English language learners (ELL) 6, 45, 52,
    63, 92–93
equality 11–12, 77, 148
everyone, LAP is for 7, 9, 46, 104–106, 146–147
explicit teaching about language 110–111

families
    challenges of working with 114–121
    in the classroom 60, 105, 118, 119
    grandparents 88–90, 91, 108, 117, 118, 153
    questionnaires for 115, 119
    resources for 118–119, 128, 155–156
    sharing family stories 50, 118–120
    sharing information about names 65–66
    supporting dual-language working 79, 85–86,
        91, 118
    understanding about bilingualism
        107–108, 117
    working with 8, 51, 77, 79, 88–90, 93–94,
        113, 114–121
Far Eastern books 155
Ferrazzi, K. 123
fieldwork 3
five 1–4
Flerspråkighet: Alla barn, alla språk, alla
    dagar! [Multilingualism: All children, all
    languages, every day!] 133–134
Flores, N. 13
food 74, 87, 90–91
foreign languages, using as a common
    language 87
formulaic expressions 22
funding for multilingual initiatives 50
funds of knowledge 12, 47

g5 1
Gaelic 59
Gallagher, E. 7, 127
games to increase participation 69
García, O. 6, 9, 11, 13, 14, 16, 81, 93
Gatt, C. xvi
Germany 70–75, 133
gesture 68, 131, 132
Gibbons, P. 12, 29
gimme five 1